HIGH-PERFORMANCE

NUTRITION FOR HIGH SCHOOL ATHLETES

A Guide for Parents and Athletes to Fuel for Maximum Performance.

BY

JUSTIN KEGLEY

Dedication:

This book is dedicated to the next generation of athletes.

I pray that you DREAM BIG, but work HARDER.

Never Be Outworked.

Be Great Today!

ISBN: 9798867258504

Imprint: Independently published

The author disclaims responsibility for adverse effects or consequences from the misapplication or injudicious use of the information contained in this book. Mention of resources and associations does not imply an endorsement.

Disclaimer

This publication is solely for informational purposes and is not a substitute for professional medical advice, diagnosis, or treatment. It is grounded in scientific research but is not designed to prevent or treat any illness. Readers should always consult with a healthcare professional before making significant dietary changes. The author holds no responsibility for any outcomes resulting from the implementation of the recommendations within. Use this information at your own risk.

TABLE OF CONTENTS

INTRODUCTION

"Tell me what you eat, and I will tell you what you are."

– G.K. Chesterton.

I love training high school athletes.

As the owner of Movement Fitness, a sports performance facility in Rockford, IL, I've had the privilege to coach thousands of athletes.

We have trained athletes who have gone on to play at Wisconsin, North Carolina, Oregon State, Illinois, Iowa, Ohio, Northeastern, not to mention the 100's of amazing DII and DIII schools.

Training athletes to reach their full GOD-given potential is a passion of mine.

We help athletes develop the physical qualities that allow them to play their sport to the best of their ability.

As a coach, my mission is to ethically help them unlock their full potential.

Our goal is to build:

- Game changing speed & agility to leave the competition in the dust.
- An explosive vertical jump for power development
- Maximal Strength to battle the competition
- Energy Systems to play longer than anyone else
- Reduce the risk of injury
- Build mental toughness to shine when the lights are bright.

There are many factors that impact a player's ability to be their best.

One topic that continually emerges as a question or statement from parents, coaches and athletes is nutrition.

- "What should I be eating?"
- "What should my daughter eat to get better but not bulky?"
- "How much protein should I be eating?"
- "What should I do to help my athlete who doesn't want to eat breakfast?"

We have made nutrition too complex.

Parents and coaches hear about new studies on what to eat, the new fad diets and how to lose weight.

We try to teach our athletes what to eat often without doing the work ourselves to SHOW athletes how to eat.

Athletes don't think skipping meals is a big deal, don't want to spend time preparing their food and are more focused on skill work and practice than eating and sleeping to fuel and recover to perform well.

Nutrition is simple, but not easy.

There are multiple factors affecting a teenager's dietary choices, such as:

- Daily schedule
- Personal preferences
- Food sensitivities
- Preparation

The Survey

Last summer, we had over 130 athletes in our program at Movement Fitness.

To better understand our athletes' nutrition habits we decided to do an unscientific survey of our athletes.

Specifically, we asked our athletes 4 questions at the beginning of their training sessions.

1. What did you eat for breakfast?
2. What did you eat before training today? (if not training first thing in the morning)
3. Have you had at least 10 oz of water today?
4. What will you eat after training?

What did you have for Breakfast?

The typical answer was:

Nothing

A granola bar

Cereal (generally sugary)

Did you eat before training today?

No.

Surprisingly, many kids came to us first thing in the morning or came straight from practice without additional nutrition or hydration to fuel their training.

Have you had at least 10 oz of water today? (Morning Training Sessions)

No.

What are you going to eat after training?

I don't know / nothing immediately

I'm going right to practice after this, so nothing.

Houston, we have a problem!

It was tough to hear.

We have incredibly dedicated young athletes backed by supportive parents.

However, their nutritional decisions are not supporting their goals.

In America, we spend thousands of dollars on extra training for sport specific skills, speed and power and more only to undermine their progress by allowing our athletes to fuel with crap!

It would be the equivalent to building a powerful sports car and fueling it with regular unleaded.

It's a waste of time, money and worst of all, potential.

Our objective is to CHANGE this!

Message to Athletes:

This guide offers you a roadmap that will clearly spell out what to eat, when to eat and why.

The majority of the information is simple, but here is an important phrase for you.

"What's simple to do is also simple not to do. The magic is not in the complexity of the task; the magic is in the doing of simple things repeatedly and long enough to ignite the miracle of the Compound Effect."

-Jim Rohn

No one is going to do this work for you.

You need to fuel yourself to play your best.

You need to wake up in time to eat breakfast.

You need to pack your lunch and after school snacks.

You need to pack your post workout / training shake or meal.

You need to put your phone down and go to bed on time.

If you want to play at the highest level possible for you, you must give your best effort in all areas.

It's not about perfection, it's about progress.

If you want to get better, you must eat well.

You must fuel your body for progress.

You are responsible for the work you put in in order to achieve your goals.

Message To Parents:

First, I'm the parent of a teenager.

I understand ALL the issues with high school athletes.

It can be VERY challenging to get them to eat well (or clean their room...)

I know you are trying to do the right things to help your child.

I know you want the best for them.

I also know that you have told them what to do lots of times.

It can be frustrating.

Nothing will ever be perfect, and it shouldn't be an expectation.

That said, I'm going to give you some truth.

Your children's eating habits *are primarily on you.*

What you allow will continue.

They don't buy the groceries.

If you don't like that they eat junk most of the time, stop buying it!

You hold tremendous power over their food choices.

Also, you lose credibility if you tell them to do one thing, then do another.

If you're harping on the importance of breakfast, but don't eat a good one yourself, it's contradictory.

If you spend your time getting drive-through more often than not because it's convenient, you are contributing to the problem.

You are willing to spend extraordinary amounts of time, energy and money to help your child achieve their goals, yet when it comes to nutrition, we allow them to eat crap.

If that's the case, you're wasting your time and money.

It's not your job to do everything, but it is your job to help guide them.

As high schoolers, they need to start taking some responsibility for their goals, but they need your guidance along the way.

You are still the biggest influence in their lives, take advantage of the opportunity to not only maximize their performance on the field, but build habits that will lead them to success in the future.

Message to Coaches:

You have a MASSIVE opportunity to speak into athletes' lives.

You don't have to have a nutrition degree or certification to help them make better choices.

Parents are ALWAYS looking for good people to speak to our kids.

This is another chance for you to help the athlete and parents while helping your athlete achieve their full potential!

Also, if you want to build mentally and physically tougher athletes, they need to fuel for it!

Make them hydrate before practice with 10-12 ounces of water.

Provide or recommend snacks for after school practices to fuel better.

Remind them to have a post practice shake or meal to fuel up.

Regular reminders can help reinforce parents' work at home and keep good nutrition habits in front of an athlete's mind!

Together, we can help make a difference for this generation that will help them become better athletes and build healthy habits for life!

Goal For This Book

My goals for this book are simple.

Create a clear, simple and specific guide to teach athletes, parents and coaches on:

- Why nutrition is key to fuel for performance and reduce injury risk

- What they should eat/ drink

- When they should eat/ drink

- How to develop the daily habits that will lead to a lifetime of improved health.

What Book Is

This book is meant to be a guide.

A roadmap for athletes, parents and coaches to help guide athletes to learn how to maximize their performance while also building healthy life habits along the way.

This book is a collection of answers to questions that I have received during my time as a coach.

In addition to that, this is directed mostly towards athletes so they can understand what is required of a high performance athlete.

It is an opportunity to help explain nutrition to athletes so they get it.

Additionally, it is a support to parents who have been telling their kids this stuff for years, but because you are mom and dad, you have no "credibility."

I am NOT a registered dietician or a nutritionist.

I am NOT addressing any medical issues or providing medical nutritional therapy.

I am a Certified Sports Nutrition Coach.

I have also held nutrition certifications from other companies such as Precision Nutrition.

For the last 15 years, I have worked with athletes to build nutrition plans that allow them to maximize performance and minimize their risk of injury!

Why Me?

This is an area that I am incredibly passionate about for numerous reasons.

As an athlete who played multiple sports in high school, as well as college football, I understand the need to fuel for performance.

After college, I grew to weigh 300 lbs, this was a low point in my life.

Once my oldest son was born, I said enough.

I went on a journey to get healthy and be the example for my family.

I was able to lose 75 lbs and have maintained that weight loss for 17 years.

That experience has helped me develop the habits and routines to maintain that weight loss, but also fuel for performance in my own life.

If you have any questions, please feel free to contact me at justin@movementfitnessrockford.com.

You can also follow me on social media:

Instagram: @coachkeg | @movement815

Facebook: www.facebook.com/jakegley

Youtube: https://www.youtube.com/@movement815

CHAPTER 1

| DEVELOPING AN UNSHAKEABLE MINDSET

"The pain of discipline is nothing like the pain of disappointment."

– Justin Langer

Be Great Today.

This is a phrase we have used for over a decade to help athletes win.

It is about being intentional with the 2 things in life that we are in complete control of:

Our Attitude and our Actions.

Ultimately, to win, you need to build a mindset that will allow you to focus and become unshakeable in the moments of challenge.

To put in the work necessary during the dark hours, the times that no one sees in order to shine when the lights are brightest.

Our life is a series of consequences for the decisions that we make.

Good or Bad, You will get OUT what you put IN!

If you want a Level 10 result, you must put in a Level 10 effort.

If you put in a level 3 effort, you will get a level 3 result.

If you want to earn a scholarship, a starting position, or make the team, you must put forth your best effort to make that happen.

We are beginning with mindset because it is the difference between someone that reaches their full potential and someone who doesn't.

We want to help athletes build the mental toughness to overcome the challenges they will face.

To develop an Unshakeable Mindset instead of an Average Mindset.

How to build an Unshakeable Mindset:

Focus on what you CAN control, not what you can't.

Say "I CHOOSE TO" instead of saying "I HAVE TO."

Focus on the STANDARD not their FEELINGS.

Find a Way, not an excuse.

Know that excellence is a lifestyle, not an event.

Show up EVERYDAY, not just GAMEDAY.

Focus on being PRESENT, not being perfect.

Believe that every "loss" is a lesson.

Has a W.I.N. Mentality (What's Important Now)

Knows that Pressure is a Privilege.

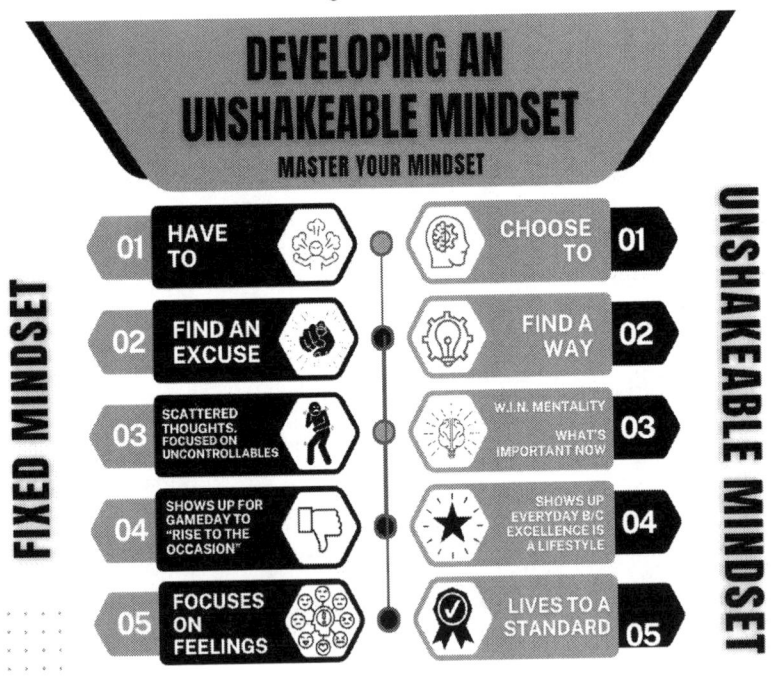

These phrases show the contrast between reaching your full potential and not.

Excellence is not complicated, but it does take consistent, focused effort.

The mind is a battleground.

Mental toughness is a matter of being able to control your thoughts.

To take control of the conversation in your mind.

Learning to talk TO yourself, not LISTEN to yourself.

To know that when you think you are done mentally, you are only about 40% done.

Understanding that the body is capable of more, but it is the mind we first have to convince.

The first key is to create a compelling vision for your future.

Understanding Your Why

Before you can build the Unshakeable Mindset, we must know WHY we are doing it.

You need to create a clear picture of what you want to achieve.

You need to get VERY clear on what you want and why.

Think of it this way: if you were going on a trip, you would need to know the destination before you started driving.

We are not going on a trip just for the journey.

We are aiming to get somewhere.

- To earn a starting spot.
- To earn a scholarship.
- To compete at our highest level.

Most people never achieve anything near their full potential because they don't know what they TRULY want.

They lose focus because we don't have clear vision or purpose.

You must know what you want if you want to achieve more.

Here's why.

Without a purpose, you will get pulled off track.

Without a vision, you will get distracted by shiny objects.

I can give you all the details of nutrition, but if you don't have the commitment and consistency to follow through with those details, then it doesn't matter.

So, the first goal of this book is for you to **create a vision board.**

Creating a Vision Board

"Champions aren't made in gyms. Champions are made from something they have deep inside of them: a desire, a dream, a vision."

-Muhammad Ali

I want you to create a vision that is so clear and compelling that looking at it will inspire and motivate you DAILY to take the actions necessary to achieve your goals.

If you have a precise picture and vivid vision, the more it will keep you on track.

Steps to Creating A Compelling Vision Board:

- **Define Clear Goals:**
  - Start by identifying specific goals.
  - These could be related to athletic performance, academic achievements, or personal growth.
  - 'Improve my vertical jump by 3".'
  - 'Maintain a GPA of 3.5 or higher.'
- **Inspirational Images and Quotes:**
  - Look for images that represent your goals.
  - Pictures of college athletes, the logos of colleges you're interested in, action shots from your sport, or images that represent personal growth and academic success.

- Also include motivational quotes that resonate with your goals.
- **Choose a Board:**
  - Select a board to serve as your vision board.
  - Poster board, corkboard, or even a digital board.
- **Arrange and Attach Your Items:**
  - Layout your images and quotes on the board that looks good and inspires you.
  - Once it looks good to you, attach them using pins, tape, or glue.
- **Build an Action Plan:**
  - Alongside the inspirational items, it's helpful to create a specific plan of action.
  - Create a specific, daily training schedule, academic plan, and a list of skills you want to develop.
    - Sport Specific Skills
      - Ball handling
      - Shooting
      - Hitting
    - Athletic Skills
      - Speed
      - Vertical Jump
      - Strength
    - Study Skills
      - Learn to read faster
      - Develop test taking strategies
- **Regular Check Ins:**
  - Update your vision board regularly
  - As you progress, add new goals, achievements, and inspirational items.

- Reflect DAILY on your progress and how your vision board has helped guide you.
- **Prominent Display:**
  - Place your vision board somewhere you will see it EVERY DAY.
  - This could be in your bedroom, a study area, or a locker.
    - Tip: A digital vision board can be copied and put in multiple places.
- **Create a Support Group:**
  - Share your vision board with your coach, family, or friends.
  - Choose people that will help hold you accountable to your goals.
- **Visualization and Affirmations:**
  - Spend time each day visualizing achieving your goals.
  - Use affirmations to reinforce an Unshakeable Mindset and belief in yourself..
- **Celebrate Progress:**
  - Don't forget to acknowledge and celebrate the progress you make toward your goals.
  - Big or small, acknowledge your wins.
  - This will help motivate you to keep going.

A vision board is a personal tool to help keep you on track.

It's also not a static tool.

It should also change and adapt overtime.

The vision board will help keep you focused on your priorities so that you can consistently put in the effort to achieve your long-term goals.

Get clear on this first.

CHAPTER 2

THE FUNDAMENTALS OF SUCCESS

"Get the fundamentals down and the level of everything you do will rise."

- Michael Jordan

Once you have a vision for your life, then you can start to reverse engineer the process to develop the habits, behaviors and routines of success.

Champions have a system, a way of doing things that allows them to show up consistently.

High school athletes tend to think that their performance only improves on the field or court.

They often neglect some key areas of their lives that will impact their success.

The habits you have will determine your success.

All of them.

"The way you do one thing is the way you do everything." – Nick Saban (use a pullout)

Athletes usually think in terms of intensity, rather than consistency.

But that's not how winning is done.

Consistency is the key to winning.

Intensity of training doesn't matter if you can't be consistent.

You must establish routines that you can execute daily.

Building your own routine is important, but we also need to remember that success leaves clues.

Let's look at some of the habits and routines of athletes that are competing at the highest levels of their capabilities.

- Set up a consistent schedule
  - Bedtime
  - Wakeup time
  - Eating schedules
  - Deliberate practice times
- Wake up early
  - Don't get on their phone before they are ready for the day
- Eat breakfast that will fuel them for success
- Read and listen to Positive Messages
  - Books
  - Podcasts
  - Music
- Train with intensity, consistently
- Have predetermined skill work goals
  - '500 shots per day"
  - '300 swings per day'
- Hold themselves accountable
- Do what is necessary, not what they FEEL like
- Do 1 more than they thought possible.
  - 1 more rep in the gym
  - 1 more conditioning drill
  - 1 more round of shooting, dribbling, hitting drills
- Stay on schedule
- Refuse to procrastinate
  - Put your phone in airplane mode when doing homework
  - Reduce phone usage

- Don't get distracted for long
- Go to bed on time to get 8+ hours of sleep regularly
  - Sleep with their phone OUTSIDE of their room
  - Put their phone away 30-60 minutes before bed.
  - Go to bed on time

Building your routine will take time and will constantly evolve as you learn and improve.

But, one thing that is important is giving your BEST effort.

Attack The Process

If you want to win, you have to attack each day.

Becoming your best is not about trophies or personal accolades.

It's about being your best.

> *"Winning is your ability to look yourself in the mirror one day at a time and say TODAY I GAVE IT MY VERY BEST."*

-Ben Newman

You must be willing to be relentless and attack each day.

You must do the work that it will take to become a CHAMPION every day.

Be Great Today.

Control your attitude and actions.

Win This Day.

Focus on your routines and execute with consistency.

When you wake up in the morning, know exactly what you are going to do.

Live life on purpose.

Remember, "what's simple to do is also simple not to do.

Winning occurs during the unseen practice and training times.

It happens in the morning, making a great breakfast when you would rather sleep 10 extra minutes.

It happens when you limit your screen time and go to bed when you should.

The BRIGHT LIGHTS will reveal your work during the DARK HOURS.

Your results will depend on your effort.

Lock in and make it happen.

CHAPTER 3

WHY FUELING FOR PERFORMANCE MATTERS

"Proper nutrition is the difference between feeling exhausted and getting the most out of a workout."

– Summer Sanders

If you have big goals, you must show up with consistency and intensity.

Achieving your goals requires consistent high-level effort, daily. (pull out)

Consistent daily high-level effort requires energy.

Energy comes from sleep and what you feed yourself.

You can't skip breakfast and expect great energy throughout your day.

You can't expect to feel energized for practice after eating a crappy lunch of bosco sticks, pizza and cheese fries.

You can't skip a snack after school, go to practice, and expect to play at a high level.

You can't expect to play in college or beyond without appropriately fueling yourself.

Our body has energy systems that play a vital role in athletic performance.

Fueling these systems for success comes from our nutrition.

Energy Systems 101:

- **ATP-PC System (Phosphagen System):**
  - This system is used for short, high-intensity bursts of activity, like sprinting or weightlifting, and lasts between 6-10 seconds.
  - It provides immediate energy through the breakdown of adenosine triphosphate (ATP) and creatine phosphate (CP) in the muscles.
  - This system is key for power production and quick bursts.
  - Foods that help replenish this system are high in creatine, such as:
    - Meats
    - Poultry
    - Fish

- **Anaerobic System:**
  - This system is used for activities that last between 30 – 120 seconds.
  - It activates when the ATP-CP system's energy is depleted.
  - It breaks down glucose without oxygen (anaerobically) for energy, producing lactic acid as a byproduct.
  - In this system, energy comes from glucose that is stored in the muscles or liver (glycogen).
  - Fueling appropriately creates food stores that allow for proper energy production during practice, training and games.
  - Carbohydrates are critical for this energy system.

- *Aerobic System*:
  - This system is crucial for long-duration, lower-intensity activities like distance running or cycling.
  - It uses oxygen to convert primarily carbohydrates and fats into energy.
  - It is used for longer duration sports such as soccer, hockey, cross country, swimming and more.
  - Carbohydrates and fats are important to fuel this energy system.

Athletes need to build a balanced diet tailored to their specific energy needs and the demands of your sport to ensure optimal performance and recovery.

Knowing what energy systems you use will help make good choices.

While proper nutrition is important for our energy systems, it is also important for other reasons.

Nutrition is also important for recovery, injury prevention, and overall health.

Here are a few ways that nutrients impact our body.

Macro and Micronutrients 101

- *Protein:*
  - Essential for muscle repair and growth.
  - Protein is crucial after exercise for recovery and to aid in the adaptation process of muscles to training.
- *Carbohydrates:*
  - The body's primary energy source.
  - Important for fueling the aerobic system and replenishing glycogen stores in muscles and the liver.
  - Athletes need a diet moderate high in carbohydrates, especially before endurance events.

- *Fats:*
  - ○ They provide a significant energy source for long-duration, low to moderate intensity exercise.
  - ○ Healthy fats are an essential part of an athlete's diet.
  - ○ They also provide important nutrients to the brain and joints.
- *Hydration:*
  - ○ Water and electrolytes are vital for maintaining hydration status, which is crucial for optimal performance and preventing fatigue and cramps.
- *Micronutrients:*
  - ○ Vitamins and minerals are essential for energy production, muscle contraction, bone health, and immunity.
  - ○ They play a role in many bodily functions crucial for athletic performance.

Nutrition for Injury Reduction

We want to utilize nutrition to minimize the risk of injury.

In sports, injuries are going to happen.

Fueling for maximum performance makes sense, but we also have to look at the other end of the spectrum.

We want to do everything we can to reduce the risk of injury, but also recuperate faster if we do get hurt.

Here are a few more ways nutrition impacts athletes.

- **Bone Health:**
  - ○ Calcium and vitamin D are vital for bone health.
  - ○ Strong bones are less prone to fractures and stress injuries, which are common in high-impact sports.

- **Energy Levels:**
  - Proper nutrition ensures a consistent energy supply.
  - This also helps athletes reduce the rate of fatigue.
- **Immune Function:**
  - A balanced diet rich in vitamins and minerals supports the immune system.
  - A strong immune system helps athletes avoid illness and recover faster from minor injuries.
- **Weight Management:**
  - Proper nutrition aids in maintaining a healthy weight.
  - Being overweight or underweight can put additional stress on the body, leading to a higher risk of injury.
- **Inflammation Reduction:**
  - Foods high in omega-3 fatty acids and antioxidants can help reduce inflammation, aiding in quicker recovery from injuries and strenuous workouts.
- **Joint Health:**
  - Nutrients like omega-3s and glucosamine can support joint health, reducing the risk of joint-related injuries, especially in sports that involve repetitive movements.
- **Recovery Time:**
  - Adequate nutrition speeds up recovery time post-injury by providing the body with the necessary nutrients to heal.

Fueling for performance and reducing the risk of injury requires time, planning, and preparation.

You can't wing it.

It takes time and intentionality to:

- Make your meals in advance
- Pack your snacks for practice after school.

- Wake up in the morning with enough time to make breakfast or drink a shake that will fuel you throughout the day.
- Communicate with your parents about the foods you want them to purchase at the store.

We want to fuel our bodies to WIN!

That goes beyond just eating enough before a game or during a tournament.

That means eating breakfast every day.

It means eating a great lunch, along with a snack after school and before practice.

It means taking in protein and carbs after a game, practice or training to begin the recovery process.

By doing that we are creating the optimal energy stores in our body so that way we can:

- Train Harder at Practice to Maximize our Skills.
- Work Harder in Training to get Faster, Jump Higher and Get Stronger
- Recover Faster after Training, Practice or Games
- Pay Attention and Retain more Information in the Classroom
- Show up every day and give a great effort

The fundamentals of nutrition are not complicated.

They are easy to achieve.

Again, what is simple to do is simple not to do.

The basics require discipline.

Missing 1 glass of water isn't a big deal once..

Skipping breakfast because you're "not hungry" won't hurt once.

Missing your after school snack isn't a problem once.

But, if you continuously miss it, it will become a big deal.

Over the long term though it IS a big deal because it leaves you groggy, tired and decreases your focus in the classroom.

It also means your body isn't getting the fuel it needs to prepare or recover for your sport.

Back to the first part of this book, getting clear on your goals.

If you want to achieve BIG goals, then BIG commitments are required.

You have to decide which player you are.

To BE GREAT means that you:

- Pay Attention to the Details
- Fuel for Performance
- Take the Warmups Seriously
- Maximize Every Rep in the Weight Room
- Study Consistently to learn, not just ace a test
- Lead by Example
- Show Up When You Don't Feel Like it
- Find a Way, Not an Excuse
- Focus on What you can Control
- Give Your BEST Every time

As an athlete, you are busy.

You have many things that are pulling on you.

Parents, coaches, teachers, friends, and more.

Achieving peak performance requires that you have the energy to show up EVERYDAY and give your BEST effort.

Too many athletes are inconsistent in their effort in large part because they don't eat well.

I want you to be able to OUTWORK the competition because you are fueled up and ready to maximize your GOD given talents with a GREAT work ethic.

CHAPTER 4

HYDRATION – QUENCHING FOR PEAK PERFORMANCE

"Water is the most neglected nutrient in your diet, but one of the most vital."

– Julia Child

The human body is made up of 60% water.

The brain and heart are 73% water, while the lungs are about 83% water.

The skin is 64% water, muscles and kidneys are 79% water, and even bones contain large amounts of water at 31%.

Water is a big deal for the human body.

The NUMBER 1 cause for decreases in performance is...*DEHYDRATION!*

Hydration is also a priority because water plays a role in every cell of our body and it's the easiest issue to fix, immediately.

Water makes up somewhere between 50 and 70% of our body.

That is significant.

It impacts your abilities on the field or court as well as in the classroom.

Proper hydration will ensure you can think and play at your highest potential.

Reasons Why Proper Hydration Matters:

- Body Temperature Regulation:
  - Hydration helps regulate body temperature.

- During exercise, the body produces heat, which is dissipated through sweat.
- Adequate fluids are necessary to maintain this sweating process.
- **Healthy Joints:**
  - Fluids help in lubricating joints, reducing the risk of joint pain and injuries which are common in sports.
- **Nutrient Transport:**
  - Hydration facilitates the transportation of nutrients and oxygen to cells, providing the energy needed for athletic performance.
- **Removing Waste:**
  - It aids in flushing out waste products from the body.
  - During intense physical activity, muscles produce waste products like lactic acid which need to be removed to prevent cramping and fatigue.
- **Focus:**
  - Hydration is important for cognitive functions such as concentration, decision-making, and reaction time, all of which are critical in sports.
- **Muscle Function:**
  - Adequate hydration is necessary for optimal muscle function and strength, as well as for preventing muscle cramps.
- **Cardiovascular Health:**
  - Proper hydration helps maintain blood volume, which is essential for efficient circulation and heart function.

We start the day slightly dehydrated and need to make up for it.

Why?

Because fluid loss, as little as 1% of our body weight, can be harmful to performance.

Here are a few ways dehydration can cause issues.

Consequences of Dehydration:

- **Decreased Mental Function:**
  - Dehydration can impair cognitive functions such as focus, alertness, and reaction time, which are important in many sports.
  - Dehydration can also cause headache, dizziness and lightheadedness.
- **Muscle Cramping & Reduced Performance:**
  - Without adequate hydration, muscles may be more prone to cramping, which reduces performance, to the point of taking them out of the game.
  - Even mild dehydration can impair physical performance, reduce endurance, and make it harder to perform high-intensity activities.
  - Athletes who are dehydrated often experience increased fatigue, both physically and mentally.
- **Overheating:**
  - Dehydration impairs the body's ability to regulate temperature, leading to overheating or heat-related illnesses like heat stroke, especially in hot and humid conditions.
- **Cardiovascular Strain:**
  - It can cause cardiovascular strain, making the heart work harder to pump blood, which can be particularly risky during intensive exercise.

For high school athletes, maintaining hydration is essential not just during sports activities but throughout the day.

Body Signals of Dehydration General – headache, fatigue, increase in heart rate	
Percent Body Water Loss by Body Weight	Progressive Effects of Dehydration
0 – 1	Thirst
2 to 5	Dry mouth, flushed skin, fatigue, headache, impaired physical performance
6	Increased body temperature, breathing rate and pulse rate
8	Dizziness, increased weakness, labored breathing with exercise
10	Muscle spasms, swollen tongue, delirium, wakefulness
11	Poor blood circulation, failing kidney function
Source: Complete Food and Nutrition Guide	

Signs of Dehydration

The first sign that you are becoming dehydrated....

You are thirsty.

Other early signs of dehydration include dry mouth, fatigue, dizziness, headaches.

You can "make up" for not drinking water at regular intervals, but it is easier to sip water throughout the day continuously.

Your body takes time to respond to the water/ hydration that goes into your system.

Waiting to drink water will decrease your performance and even cost you playing time because of cramps or poor performance.

You can't expect to drink a little water or electrolyte drink and just be ok.

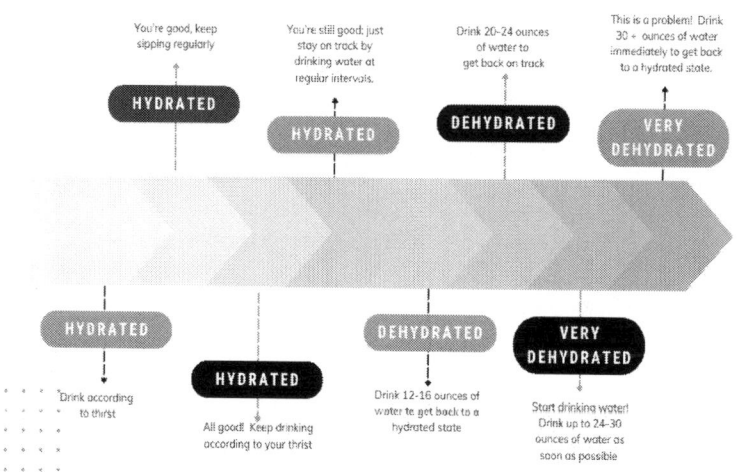

ATHLETE HYDRATION CHART

ARE YOU DEHYDRATED

You're good, keep sipping regularly	You're still good: just stay on track by drinking water at regular intervals.	Drink 20-24 ounces of water to get back on track	This is a problem! Drink 30 + ounces of water immediately to get back to a hydrated state.
HYDRATED	**HYDRATED**	**DEHYDRATED**	**VERY DEHYDRATED**

HYDRATED	**HYDRATED**	**DEHYDRATED**	**VERY DEHYDRATED**
Drink according to thirst	All good! Keep drinking according to your thrist	Drink 12-16 ounces of water to get back to a hydrated state	Start drinking water! Drink up to 24-30 ounces of water as soon as possible

Another way you can tell if you are dehydrated is to go to the bathroom.

Based on the color of your urine, you will be able to see whether you are dehydrated or not in real time.

In the graphic below, you can see 3 brackets with multiple levels to each.

The first bracket means you are well-hydrated and you can drink according to your thirst levels.

The second bracket means that you are starting to get dehydrated.

While you are certainly not in danger of a medical issue, you will start feeling the effects we discussed earlier.

To get rehydrated you would need to drink approximately 12-20 ounces of water.

That will get you back on track quickly.

Getting into the last bracket is where you can start to have issues.

If you have dark-colored urine, you will need to get a large amount of water in you quickly.

Also, if you are hydrated, you should be making regular trips to the bathroom.

It shouldn't interrupt your day, but it should be enough that you have to go consistently throughout the day.

To avoid dehydration, make sure you are consistently drinking enough water.

How much should I drink?

The simplest equation for water consumption is this:

Drink ½ your body weight in ounces + 15 per day.

That is on a standard day, with little to moderate activity.

On days that include practices, training or games, most athletes should drink 100 oz of water.

What to drink

Now, you need to know that hydration includes more than just water.

First, WATER should be the primary source of hydration.

It is the BEST source of hydration when you are not competing.

Sports drinks have grown in popularity, and companies have even created ways to make them lower calories.

Still, the point of a sports drink is to replace electrolytes when you are playing and provide some energy in the form of carbohydrates.

If you're not sweating, you don't need a sports drink!

If you are at school, there is no need to drink anything but water.

It will make your life easier.

Find a water bottle and carry it around with you all day.

Know how many ounces you have in a water bottle, then drink accordingly.

A Stanley or Hydro flask-type bottle holds 30-40 ounces of water.

If you weigh 150 pounds, you need 90 oz of water because that's half your body weight plus 15.

You need to drink approximately 3 of those.

Pretty simple.

Sports Drinks

You don't need a sports drink if you're not TRAINING HARD for at least an hour.

Period.

Sports drinks are designed to add electrolytes, carbohydrates and flavor.

The goal is that they would quickly replenish your system and allow you to maintain a higher level of energy and performance.

Here's what we recommend.

You can use LMNT, Liquid IV, or Gatorade.

These products all offer the appropriate sodium and potassium levels to help replenish our system.

They also have flavors that encourage "chugging" because if you are genuinely dehydrated or on the verge of dehydration, you must get fluids into your body quickly.

I don't recommend any sports drinks that offer less than 100 mg of sodium per serving..

In order to replenish electrolytes, we need to focus on sodium.

We need sodium more than potassium in gametime scenarios.

We don't want to have high sodium products all the time, but in this instance, in a game where you're playing for extended periods, you want the sodium because it's an important part of the electrolyte profile.

I don't recommend the low calorie or zero-calorie version of these drinks.

While they are low carb and have electrolytes, they are not as clean a product and have dyes in them that aren't desired.

Plus, if you are not sweating, there is no need to replace electrolytes.

Water is more than enough in our everyday life, and it's significantly cheaper for parents.

Parents, feel free to spend money on flavored drinks if you want, but know it is not necessary.

Caffeine

I don't believe anyone under 18 should drink caffeine.

Period.

Kids need sleep.

They need to learn to recover.

High school athletes need to learn to prioritize the important things, put the phone down at night and go to bed on time.

Caffeine is one of the most popular drugs in America.

Adults use caffeine to mask poor sleep, nutrition, and lifestyle management habits.

The American Academy of Pediatrics says stimulant-containing energy drinks have no place in the diets of children or adolescents.

The AAP officially recommends less than 100 milligrams of caffeine a day.

Athlete's bodies aren't prepared to absorb it the same way an adult does.

They're still developing.

Sleeping 9-11 hours will provide you with the energy you need.

Caffeine just masks our lack of sleep or recovery.

Don't drink caffeine.

Drinking caffeine impacts our energy and central nervous system.

It allows you to exert more energy in the short term but also impacts energy management later.

It will affect what time you go to bed.

That, in turn, impacts how late you get up.

Then, traditionally, you are tired and therefore reach for more caffeine.

It can be a vicious cycle

Given that 60 to 70% of high school and middle school students don't get enough sleep already, drinking caffeine can worsen your sleeping pattern.

Caffeine consumption can also increase anxiety and nervousness.

Given the mental health issues we are battling today, the last thing we need is to encourage more anxiety through the consumption of caffeine.

Plus, soda, energy drinks, and coffee all have MAJOR downfalls.

Too much sugar or additives will impact your athlete's long-term health.

A GREAT life habit is getting your kids to learn to drink water as their MAIN SOURCE of hydration!

The bottom line is don't drink caffeinated or energy drinks.

How to Drink 100+ oz of Water Daily:

- **Morning Start:**
  - Begin the day with 16-20 oz of water right after waking up to kick-start hydration.
- **Scheduled Intervals:**
  - Set a reminder to drink water every hour.
  - If you aim to drink 8 oz every hour (while awake for 12 hours), you'll have consumed 96 oz by the end of the day.
- **Meals and Snacks:**
  - Always drink water with meals and snacks.
  - Aim for at least 8-12 oz.

- **Hydration Packs/Bottles:**
  - o Invest in a good water bottle or hydration pack, especially if you're in sports that have long durations or are outdoor-based, like running, cycling, or hiking.
- **Monitor Urine:**
  - o Aim for light yellow urine.
  - o If it's clear, you might be overhydrated.
  - o If it's dark, you might need to drink more.
    - ▪ *Remember that individual water needs vary based on various factors, including the specific sport, intensity, duration, body size, and environmental conditions. Adjustments might be necessary, and it's always a good idea to consult with a sports nutritionist or doctor to ensure the best hydration practices are tailored to individual needs.*

Hydration Protocols

In preparation for games, practices and training, here is the hydration protocol we follow to maximize performance and reduce the risk of injury.

- **2 hours before:**
  - o Consume 16-20 oz of water.
- **20 minutes before:**
  - o Sip on 8-12 oz.
- **During:**
  - o Every 10-15 minutes, drink 7-10 oz of water or an electrolyte solution. (Gatorade, LMNT...)
- Post activity:
  - o Rehydrate with 20-24 oz for every pound of body weight lost during the activity.

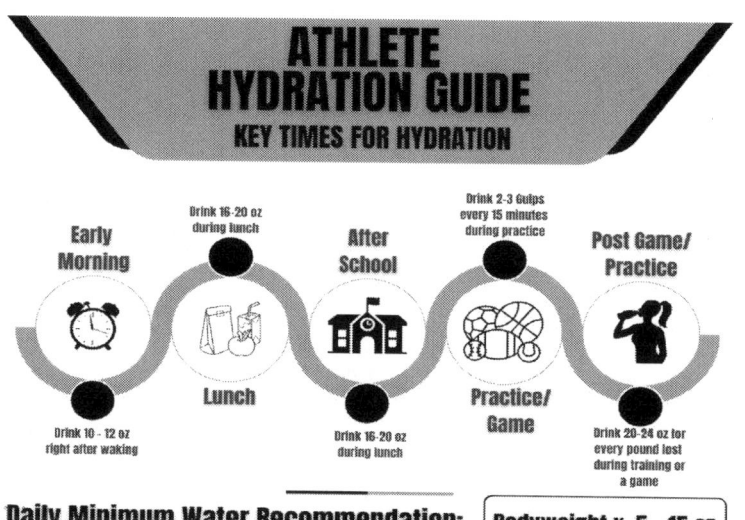

ATHLETE HYDRATION GUIDE

KEY TIMES FOR HYDRATION

Early Morning
Drink 10 - 12 oz right after waking

Lunch
Drink 16-20 oz during lunch

After School
Drink 16-20 oz during lunch

Practice/ Game
Drink 2-3 Gulps every 15 minutes during practice

Post Game/ Practice
Drink 20-24 oz for every pound lost during training or a game

Daily Minimum Water Recommendation: | Bodyweight x .5 + 15 oz

**Add more on days with practices and games.

Hydration is simple but not easy.

The reason is because it takes continuous effort.

It is easy to drink water at regular intervals most of the time.

But what is simple to do is also simple not to do because it doesn't feel like a big deal.

So prioritize hydration in your planning throughout the week and your days.

CHAPTER 5

PROTEIN — BUILDING AND REPAIRING MUSCLE

"Protein is essential for virtually every one of your cellular functions."

- Dr. Gabrielle Lyon

Our goal for athletes is to maximize speed and power while reducing the risk of injury.

Building lean muscle tissue is essential for athletes.

Often, when people hear muscle building, they think of getting "bulky."

This does NOT have to be the case, especially for female athletes.

Athlete training looks different then bodybuilding.

Athletes don't do chest, back or leg days.

They sprint, jump, and perform more whole-body movements.

Athletes develop power through explosive movements like sprinting and jumping.

Athletes utilize traditional lifts, such as squats, deadlifts and bench press to help build strength.

We want to build lean muscle tissue that will improve our bodies metabolism, while allowing athletes to compete at their highest level.

Athletes can and should gain muscle without adding significant bulk.

(If you are an athlete that is looking to bulk, you can do that through increased calories).

Muscle is essential for producing power and force.

Combining good training with protein is THE way that athletes build lean muscle.

A great way to think of protein is to imagine they are Lego's.

Protein is made up of a series of amino acids.

Just as stacking Lego bricks together to create a design, amino acids stack together to build and repair muscle tissue.

Protein helps repair our muscles after they are torn down during practices, games, and training.

In addition to that, when paired with resistance training, builds lean muscle tissue so that athletes get faster, stronger and reduce their risk of getting injured.

Consistently providing your body with protein is essential.

Unlike carbohydrates and fat, protein is not stored in the body.

Every game, practice, and training is catabolic, meaning our muscles get torn down during the process.

We need to build back up what we've torn down, and we focus on protein to rebuild our muscles.

Eating protein is not just important after a game or practice; we want to eat it regularly throughout the day.

Our goal is to ensure that we consistently provide our body with the nutrients it needs.

While eating protein is essential for performance, it is not necessary to over consume protein.

More does not equal better.

So, we want to ensure that we provide the right amount at regular intervals.

For athletes, our goal is to eat between .7 – 1 g per pound of body weight per day.

Here is how you can break that down.

(Athlete Weight) x (.7 to 1) = Total Range of Protein

Examples:

- 120 lbs. athlete x (.7 to 1) = 84 – 120 g of protein per day.

- 150 lbs. athlete x (.7 to 1) = 105 – 150 g of protein per day.

- 200 lbs. athlete x (.7 to 1) = 140 – 200 g of protein per day.

So, when we know how much protein we need to eat in a day, we want to break that out over our day in meals.

The recommended amount of protein per meal for athletes is 20 – 30 grams.

The maximum recommended amount is 40g.

After 40 g, there is no additional benefit.

As we discussed, protein is not stored in the body, so what is not used is excreted.

More is not always better.

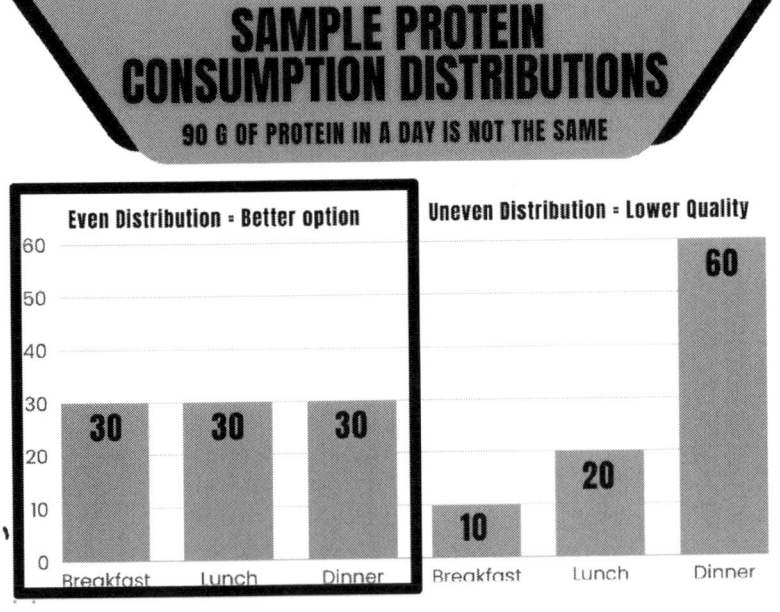

Dr. Doug Paddon- Jones, University of Texas Medical Branch

40

Now that we know how much an athlete should consume throughout the day, calculate protein needs per meal.

Let's take the 150 lbs. athlete from above.

We know they need between 105 – 150 g of protein per day.

They can eat between 4-6 meals or snacks per day.

Let's break down the math.

- (105 – 150) / 4 meals = 26 g – 37 g per meal
- (105 – 150) / 5 meals = 21 g – 30 g per meal
- (105 – 150) / 6 meals = 17 g – 25 g per meal
    - (These are rounded numbers; being exact is not necessary.)

The more frequent your meals, the less you need to eat.

The less frequent your meals, the more you need to eat.

Types of Protein

When we look at protein, there are a few different types of protein:

Complete, incomplete and complementary.

Complete proteins

Complete proteins contain all nine essential amino acids that aren't produced in our body.

We must get them from our food.

Complete proteins include:

- Chicken
- Fish
- Turkey
- Milk
- Eggs

- Quinoa

These foods supply ALL the essential amino acids.

Incomplete proteins

Incomplete proteins are food sources that contain amino acids but lack one or more of the essential amino acids.

Incomplete proteins include:

- Nuts
- Seeds
- Whole Grains
- Vegetables
- Legumes

A vegan/ vegetarian diet consists of incomplete proteins.

Complementary Proteins

- Peanuts and Almonds
- Nut Butter and Whole Grain Toast
- Beans and Rice

Complementary proteins are two or more proteins that are paired together to provide all the essential amino acids, which creates a complete protein.

Athletes who consume a vegan diet must find ways to combine multiple incomplete proteins to ensure they get all the essential amino acids they need to repair and build lean muscle tissue appropriately.

The key to Eating Protein

The key to eating more protein is planning!

We have a PROTEIN FIRST mindset when it comes to nutrition.

Protein First

- **First thing when planning your meals**
  - Protein should be in the center of your plate.
  - If you don't start with protein, it's easy to fill up on carbs and fat and not get enough protein in your system.
  - Learn to build your meals around protein. For Example
    - 'For dinner, we are going to have chicken and...'
    - 'For breakfast, we are going to have eggs and...'
    - 'For lunch, I'm going to have a turkey sandwich and...'
  - Start planning your meals around protein to help you get enough in throughout the day.
- **First thing in the morning**
  - Given that protein isn't stored in your body, we want to feed our bodies appropriately.
  - Consuming protein to start the day will allow you to continue to repair, recover, and rebuild your muscles.
    - Assist in the recovery process from last night's practice, training or games.
    - Continue to build lean muscle tissue.
  - This not only helps as an athlete as they are young, but it also helps to keep your metabolism running efficiently later in life.
- **First thing following a workout**
  - We want to begin the repair process immediately following practice, training or games and protein is the key to that.
  - Immediate consumption of protein is a great habit to get into following vigorous activity.

- There is no magic window of time, but we do recommend within 30-45 minutes of training.
  - Great Choices Include:
    - Chocolate Milk
    - Protein shakes with high quality protein
    - Meals with lean meat and carbohydrates.

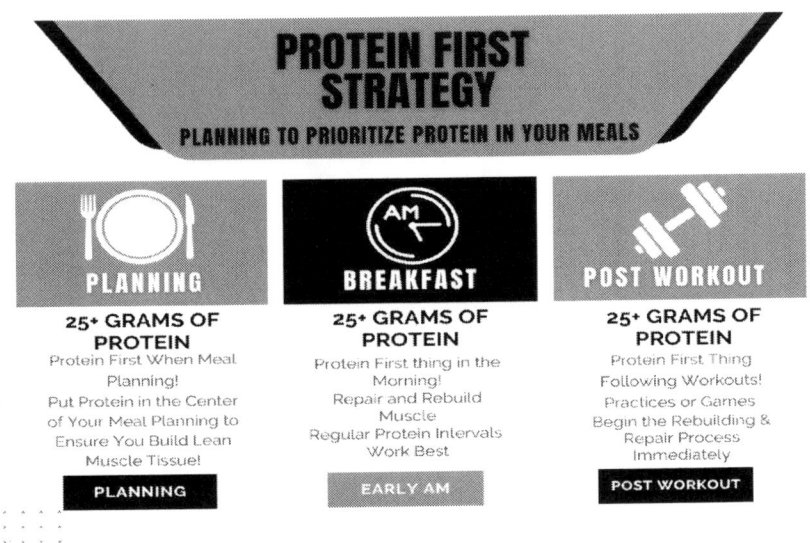

Planning for protein consumption:

Protein can be a pain because many complete proteins take time to prepare.

The easiest way to make sure that you have enough is to cook large quantities of protein in advance!

This will help athletes make better choices in the moment when they go to the fridge.

Cook up ground beef, chicken, fish, and turkey so there aren't any excuses.

If you start thinking about protein first and have protein prepared in advance, it increases the likelihood of an athlete eating protein, rather than just a low calorie snack.

Protein Powder

Is protein powder okay for my athlete?

YES!

We want the majority of our nutrition to come from whole food sources, but we know it is not always that easy.

You can and should use protein powder to **supplement** your athlete's protein needs.

Just make sure it is from a reputable company.

This should not become a crutch, athletes don't need 3 of them daily.

The goal would be to use one following a workout, game or practice.

Protein shakes are potentially a great way to start the day for those that don't want to eat in the morning.

If you have an athlete looking to gain weight, you could add another shake throughout the day.

What to eat.

In terms of what to eat, keep it simple.

Our goal is to increase the amount of whole foods and reduce the amount of processed foods.

Below, we will cover the foods we should Eat More of and Less of.

The goal is not to eliminate the foods on the eat less list.

It is exactly what it states, eat less.

Lean, whole-food protein sources will be your best option, and you can supplement with protein powders or bars occasionally.

Eat More:

- Boneless, Skinless Chicken Breast
- Roast Turkey
- Lean Beef
  - 90% Lean
  - Tenderloin
  - Flank
  - Roast
- Eggs / Egg Whites
- Fish
  - Cod
  - Flounder
  - Salmon
  - Tuna
- Milk
  - Whole Milk for those looking to add weight
  - 2% for those looking to control weight
  - Chocolate Milk post workout
- Yogurt
- Cottage Cheese
- Pork

Eat Less:
- Fried Fish
- 85% Beef
  - Unless looking to add weight
- Processed Meats
- Hot Dogs
- Chicken Strips
- Chicken Wings

Protein is essential for athletes to build and repair lean muscle tissue.

If we want to not only maximize performance but also minimize injury risk, eating good, whole food proteins consistently will be the key.

{If you are looking for a high-quality protein that tastes great and is cost-effective, try our Movement Supps brand here!}

https://movementfitnesssupplements.com/products/whey-protein

CHAPTER 6

CARBOHYDRATES – OUR MAIN SOURCE OF ENERGY

"The lack of carbohydrates can make you a little crazy."

- Tom Hardy

Carbohydrates often get a bad rap.

I understand why.

The overconsumption of carbs undoubtedly has been a major contributor to a decrease in our overall health in America.

But carbohydrates are critical for athletes who are training, practicing, and playing games consistently.

CARBOHYDRATES ARE OUR BODIES' MAIN SOURCE OF ENERGY.

Carbs power every move & everything we do.

Carbs are broken down in glucose, which powers every field and court sport that consists of short bursts. (Volleyball, Basketball, Soccer, Hockey, Football, Baseball, Tennis, Softball…)

Glucose is also vital because that is also what our brain uses for energy.

The brain uses up to 70% of the available glucose in our system.

So, if we don't have enough glucose in our system, we can start to see detrimental effects on performance and behavior.

Symptoms like:

- Brain fog
- Fatigue

- Dizziness
- Irritability

If we are not fueling our high school athletes appropriately, we will see an increase in hormones at a time when athletes already struggle to control hormones.

We must have enough carbohydrates in our system to fuel our performance.

What should we eat, and when

Carbs for athletes can be tricky.

We want to ensure that most carbohydrates come from quality, complex carbohydrates.

But there are also times when simple carbohydrates are highly beneficial for their recovery as an athlete.

Just because something is simple doesn't mean it's automatically bad.

Simple is equated with sugar, and the presumption is that sugar is bad.

I don't think so.

Is too much sugar a problem, absolutely!

But, as an athlete, utilizing some simple carbohydrates can help fuel us with fuel more quickly than complex carbohydrates.

We want to utilize a simple carbohydrate before, during, and after games, training, and practices.

Simple carbs are metabolized quickly and can be turned into fuel faster than complex carbs.

Simple carbohydrates, like those found in sports drinks, are also beneficial during the game to help the athlete fuel up for the rest of the event.

After games, training, and practice, simple carbs combined with protein within 30 minutes of completion will increase the athlete's ability to repair broken-down muscle tissues and improve recovery.

Simple carbs can look like:

- Bagels
- Fruits
- Cereal with low-fat milk
- Sports drinks
- Granola bars
- Smoothie made with fruit
- Fruit juice
- Low-fat yogurt
- Frozen yogurt

The key to this type of fueling is we don't want to combine it with highly fatty foods.

Fat slows digestion, and in the moments that we need fuel the most, we do not want to slow down the absorption of carbohydrates.

Fueling for the long-term

While we know simple carbohydrates make up energy strategies before, during, and after the competition, most of the time, we want to focus on fueling with high-quality, complex carbohydrates.

- Fruits
  - Apples
  - Berries
  - Oranges
  - Kiwi

- Vegetables
  - Sweet potatoes
  - Potatoes
  - Broccoli
  - Green beans
  - Carrots
  - Asparagus
- Whole grains
  - Oats
  - Quinoa
  - Brown rice
  - Black beans

This is a partial list, but it is a good starting point.

Complex carbohydrates allow our athletes to build a comprehensive energy system to help them perform at their peak.

Fueling for performance means eating well MOST of the time, not just the 12 hours before or after a game.

We don't need large "carb loads" for most sports.

Meals at regular intervals with carbohydrates will work just fine.

Recovery is essential.

If we do not have appropriate energy stores, none of the "simple" carbs will help.

The goal is to teach athletes to eat complete meals and supply them with the energy they need to fuel their day and performance.

For example, breakfast should be a larger meal to set us up for the day.

This will help us "break the fast" we have been in with our sleep and fuel them for the start of the day.

The challenge with breakfast for most athletes is the early morning time frame.

Teenagers generally are not early risers.

Finding meals that they will eat, as well as providing the nutrients they need, is essential.

Foods like:

- Oatmeal
- Overnight Oats
- Whole Grain Toast / Tortillas
- Quinoa
- Granola
- Fruit

Next, we have lunch.

This is difficult because some athletes eat lunch at school, and others pack their lunch.

Either way, this meal deserves discussion continually because parents have less control over the food options and athletes must make good choices at school or during summer break.

So, the goal is to help athletes prepare their food in advance to have the best options possible.

Packing their lunch will always help you to encourage your athlete to make good choices.

From a carbohydrate perspective, lunch can include:

- Wraps
- Whole Grain Bread
- Fruit
- Vegetables
- Baked Chips
- Rice (packed in thermos)

- Pasta (packed in thermos)

Any combination of these will allow you to fuel your athlete for the remainder of school, just before practice or game.

Dinner is the last "big" meal of the day.

Ideally, dinner is prepared and eaten at home.

I understand that life is busy, but this is the best way.

Mostly, dinner happens sometime after practice and before bedtime.

If dinner happens earlier, around 5 p.m., the athlete may need a snack or another meal later in the day.

Eating later is acceptable for athletes.

The goal is for it not to be junk, but if they are playing or practicing, they must eat after practice.

Again, we want to make the BEST choices possible consistently.

Dinner can include:

- Brown Rice
- Quinoa
- Sweet Potatoes
- Potatoes
- Oats
- Whole Grain Pasta
- Beans
- Spaghetti Squash
- Yogurt
- Fruit
- Vegetables
- Sprouted Breads

The goal is to help recover from the game, practice, or training and rebuild the energy stores that were depleted through those events.

The goal is never perfection, but parents have a significant influence on the behaviors of the athlete.

- What groceries are you buying?
- How much fast food are you allowing/ buying?
- Do you prepare food in advance?

Building great habits for yourself will help trickle down into your athlete and allow them to reach their full potential on the field or court and in the classroom.

Simple carbohydrates work in and around training, games, and practice to refuel and energize our athletes quickly. Still, the bottom line of carbohydrates is that we should use complex carbohydrates to fuel our bodies.

What to eat.

In terms of what to eat, here we will cover the foods we should Eat More of and Less of.

Our goal is to increase the amount of whole foods and reduce the amount of processed foods, especially for carbohydrates.

The goal is not to eliminate the foods on the eat less list.

We know that high school athletes are not going to have a perfect diet and that is not the goal.

The goal is to learn how to eat well and do that most of the time.

It is exactly what it states, eat more and eat less.

Eat More:
- Root Vegetables
  - Sweet Potatoes
  - White Potatoes

- o Squash
- o Carrots
- Whole Grains
  - o Brown Rice
  - o Quinoa
  - o Whole Wheat Pasta
  - o Couscous
  - o Wild Rice
  - o Whole Wheat Bread
  - o Bagels
  - o English Muffins
- Popcorn
- Beans
- Dairy
  - o Has protein, carbs and fat
- Fruits
  - o Bananas
  - o Apples
  - o Pears
  - o Oranges
  - o Berries
- Vegetables
  - o Green Beans
  - o Asparagus
  - o Broccoli
  - o And more…

Eat Less:

- White Breads
- Candy
- Sugary Drinks

- Soda
- Fruit Drinks
- Energy Drinks
- Cookies
- Table Sugar
- Brownies
- French Fries
- Pop Tarts
- Candy Bars

CHAPTER 7

FATS – BRINGING BALANCE TO THE BRAIN AND BODY

"Proper nutrition is the key to unlock your body's potential."

- Brian Holifield

Fats are often misunderstood and sometimes undervalued for athletes.

The name alone causes concern among many.

The belief that is often accepted is that fats will make you fat.

This couldn't be farther from the truth.

Fats are essential in an athlete's diet, especially for high school athletes.

They play a crucial role in not just sustaining energy during an athlete's training and competitions, but they also in enhancing their overall performance, recovery, and health.

Fats are an essential part of the cellular functions and hormonal balance in teenagers.

Why are Fats Important to High School Athletes

These are just a few of the reasons that fats are crucial for high school athletes.

- Energy Source:
    - Fats are a dense source of energy, providing 9 calories per gram, more than DOUBLE the energy provided by carbohydrates or proteins.

- Specifically, they're important for endurance sports where the body depends on fat stores for long-term energy.
- **Essential Fatty Acids:**
    - The body doesn't produce certain omega-3 and omega-6 fatty acids, which are essential for health.
    - These fatty acids are involved in numerous body functions, including
        - Brain development
        - Inflammation control
        - Blood clotting
- **Vitamin Absorption:**
    - Fats are necessary for the absorption of fat-soluble vitamins
        - A, D, E, and K.
        - These vitamins are important for:
            - Bone health
            - Blood clotting
            - Antioxidants
- **Hormone Production and Regulation:**
    - Fats play a key role in hormone production and regulation.
    - Specifically, hormones like:
        - Testosterone:
            - Important for muscle growth and strength.
        - Cortisol:
            - The "stress hormone" helps the body respond to stress.
            - Fats, especially cholesterol, are involved in the synthesis of cortisol.

- Thyroid Hormones:
  - Fats are important for the proper functioning of the thyroid gland, which produces hormones regulating:
    - Metabolism
    - Energy generation
    - Body temperature
- Growth Hormone:
  - Fatty acids have been shown to influence the secretion of growth hormone.
  - Important for
    - Growth
    - Body composition
    - Cell repair
    - Metabolism

- **Insulation and Protection:**
  - Fats help in insulating the body and protecting vital organs.
  - Important for athletes who play contact sports or train in cold environments.
- **Satiety and Taste:**
  - Fats contribute to feeling full after eating.
  - They also enhance the taste of food, helping to maintain a balanced diet and preventing overeating.
- **Energy Storage:**
  - Excess energy from food is stored as fat in the body.
  - This stored energy is an energy bank during prolonged physical activity or between meals.
- **Brain Health:**
  - Fats, especially omega-3 fatty acids, are essential for brain health and cognitive function.

- This is critical for high school athletes who need to balance academic and athletic demands.
- **Joint Health:**
  - Omega-3 fatty acids help reduce inflammation in the body.
  - This includes joint inflammation, which is beneficial for field and court sport athletes who put a lot of stress on their joints.

Fats are very important in the diet of a high school athlete.

Consuming the right amount of fat will allow athletes to recover faster and play longer.

High-quality fatty foods can also help maintain joint health, which is critical for an athlete.

This is extremely important for athletes who play sports that heavily impact their ankles, knees, hips, and back through excessive running, jumping, and landing.

FATS DO NOT MAKE YOU FAT (Unless you overeat.)

One common misconception is that eating fatty foods will make you fat.

As with all macronutrients, we need specific amounts to help athletes grow as humans and perform at their highest potential.

But, if we consume too many calories, we will put on weight.

It is essential to know the different types of fatty foods, which ones to consume more and which to drink less or cut out completely.

The goal should be to get most of your food from unsaturated fats, polyunsaturated and monounsaturated.

Polyunsaturated Fatty Foods:

- **Omega 6**
  - Sunflower Oil

- ○ Soybean Oil
- ○ Corn Oil
- ○ Meat
- ○ Poultry
- ○ Fish
- **Omega 3**
  - ○ Fish Oil
  - ○ Flaxseed
  - ○ Chia Seeds
  - ○ Walnuts
  - ○ Supplement Pills

Monounsaturated Fatty Foods:

- Nuts
- Nut Butters
- Olives
- Avocados
- Olive Oil
- Seeds
- Tahini

We want to limit saturated fats because they may increase the risk of heart disease. A diet heavy in saturated fats has been shown to increase LDL, also known as the "bad cholesterol.

Now, as we have mentioned before, the goal is not perfection.

The goal is to fuel the body for performance and teach good habits for life.

Saturated Fatty Foods:

- Skin On Poultry

- Visible fat on Beef
- Butter
- Cheese
- Cream
- Ice Cream
- Palm Oil

Athletes, we certainly understand and expect that you are going to eat some pizza, ice cream and other non healthy foods at times.

We want athletes and parents to understand that having these foods is okay sometimes.

There is a difference between having foods we enjoy sometimes and overeating them.

If you are serious about your sport, you can't just eat poorly and expect to perform.

You have to be willing to put in the work to prepare food that is going to fuel your body for performance rather than just eating whatever is convenient.

If your typical diet is filled with healthy, colorful foods and great protein options, then eating some pizza and ice cream occasionally won't be that big of a deal.

If they become your way of life, it will impact your body weight and overall health.

Supplements

As stated before, our goal is to get the most nutrients out of our food if possible.

We also know that it takes work to get teenagers to eat enough of the foods they need to fuel their performance.

Getting the appropriate amount of omega-3's and omega-6's through their diet is challenging.

One way to ensure your athlete gets the brain and joint health they need is through supplementation.

Taking an omega-3 vitamin supplement is one easy way that your athlete can ensure they are fueling for performance.

Omega-3 will help counteract the inflammation in our typical American diet and fuel their brain.

Since the brain is 60% fat, this is a tremendous way to ensure that our athletes get the necessary nutrients.

According to Science for Sport, omega-3s are great for recovery.

"Omega-3s contain anti-inflammatory properties, which aid in muscle recovery and injury prevention. Consuming higher omega-3s improves the integrity of your cells and cellular function, ultimately reducing muscular damage. Just seven days of supplementation can decrease post-exercise muscle damage and soreness. Additionally, omega-3s have been shown to improve sleep, a vital piece of the puzzle for performance recovery."

For high school athletes, the NIH recommends the following:

- 1.6 g of omega-3's per day for males.
- 1.1 g of omega-3's per day for females.

Fats, omega 3's in particular, are essential to our athlete's brain development. We want to ensure that they get the nutrients they need to live their best life and play to their full potential.

Omega 3's for Concussions

Fats have also recently been shown to help in the event of brain injuries such as concussions or post-concussion syndromes.

Concussions have become more a prevalent part of our sports world.

A concussion can have a significant and lasting impact on our athletes.

We want to ensure we are doing EVERYTHING possible to prevent and treat a concussion.

Consuming enough omega 3's is crucial for both pre and post-concussion.

Sport Safe, a pediatric physician lead organization and a leader in concussion treatment for athletes, says,

"Our omega-3 deficiency puts us at increased risk of a difficult recovery from a concussion. The omega-3 role in the brain is to protect brain cells, decrease inflammation, and help to improve communication between nerve cells. They can only fill these needs when the person is consuming the necessary quantity of omega-3. When a concussion occurs, if the brain is deficient in omega-3 fatty acids, it is much harder for the brain to heal itself. Additionally, research has shown that after concussion, there is a decreased amount of the omega-3 DHA in the brain tissue. Therefore, sufficient omega-3 intake is essential not only for normal brain function, but especially for the brain recovering from concussion.

There are two crucial types of Omega 3's.

EPA – Eicosapentaenoic acid

DHA – Docosahexaenoic acid

These two are required for our body to function correctly and benefit our brain, heart, skin, and almost every cell.

Medicine & Science and Sport and Exercise published a study in which they examined different dosing of DHA in collegiate American football athletes over the course of a season.

When given 2, 4 or 6 g DHA/day the researchers found an increase in blood markers for DHA in each group.

More specifically, findings from this study, the first large-scale study examining potential prophylactic use of DHA in American football athletes examined different dosing of omega 3 fats and a particular indicator of brain trauma, called neurofilament light (NFL).

NFL increases as the number of physical impacts increase.

In other words, the more hits on the field, the more NFL in the blood. But the question was can increasing DHA levels in the body reduce NFL (e.g., protect against brain trauma).

What the researchers found was those subjects on DHA supplements had a 40% reduction in NFL compared to those taking placebo.

This discovery led the researchers to conclude that it "*may indicate that DHA can be protective against some brain trauma.*"

The thought is that DHA may work by protecting athlete's brains by preventing inflammation associated with injuries.

So whether it is in the prevention of concussions or maximizing sport performance and minimizing injury risk , fats are essential for the development of a teenager.

What to eat.

In terms of what to eat, here we will cover the foods we should Eat More of and Less of.

Our goal is to increase the amount of whole foods and reduce the amount of processed foods, especially for fatty foods.

The goal is not to eliminate the foods on the eat less list.

We know that high school athletes are not going to have a perfect diet and that is not the goal.

The goal is to learn how to eat well and do that most of the time.

It is exactly what it states, eat more and eat less.

Eat More:
- Olive Oil
- Avocado
- Nuts
- Almonds
- Pistachios
- Walnuts

- Pecans
- Peanuts
- Nut Butters
  - Almond
  - Peanut
- Whole Eggs
- Avocado Oil
- Sees
  - Flax
  - Chia

Eat Less:

- Butter
- Peanut Oil
- Mayonnaise
- Ice Cream
- Skin on Poultry
- Baked Goods
- Cookies
- Brownies
- Biscuits
- Fried Foods
- Excessive Visible Fat on Meat

CHAPTER 8

BREAKFAST – FUELING THE DAY

"Breakfast is everything. The beginning, the first thing. It is the mouthful that is the commitment to a new day.

- A.A. Gill

Breakfast is ESSENTIAL for athlete's that want to play at a high level.

Breakfast means breaking the fast.

When we wake up in the morning, our body has been fasting during sleep.

We have ideally been sleeping for 8+ hours, so BREAKFAST is the time to put the nutrients into your body to fuel the day.

This can be challenging for teenagers for a variety of reasons.

Eating breakfast can be challenging for high school athletes due to several factors:

- **Early Training Sessions:**
  - Early morning training sessions without proper planning can leave you without a good breakfast..
- **Appetite Issues in the Morning:**
  - Some athletes have a lower appetite in the morning.
  - This can be exacerbated by nervousness or anxiety about the day ahead, especially before competitions.
  - Some athletes may avoid eating before training or competitions due to concerns about digestive discomfort or the fear of feeling heavy or sluggish.

- **Poor Time Management:**
  - Athletes often stay up late due to homework, social media and other activities, leading to insufficient sleep.
  - Procrastination can lead to late nights or early mornings, which cut into breakfast time.
  - This can result in difficulty waking up early enough to eat breakfast.
- **Lack of Awareness/ Nutritional Misinformation:**
  - Some athletes are not aware of the importance of breakfast for their performance and overall health.
  - Misconceptions about diet and performance, such as the belief that fasting can enhance performance or that certain foods should be avoided, might lead athletes to skip breakfast.
  - This leads to poor fueling, which impacts performance.
- **Boring Breakfast Options:**
  - Limited or unappealing breakfast choices can make the meal less enticing, especially if there's a lack of variety over time.
  - This is a lack of planning and preparation

These challenges require a combination of education about the importance of breakfast, planning strategies (like preparing breakfast ahead of time), and finding quick, easy, and delicious breakfast options that suit the athlete's tastes and nutritional needs.

I believe that breakfast is the highest-priority meal because it fuels the day.

Scientifically, as long as athletes get all the nutrients and calories they need daily, it doesn't matter when they eat.

But I still HIGHLY RECOMMEND that athletes eat breakfast.

If you are an athlete and you are choosing not to eat breakfast, it will negatively impact your ability to reach your full potential.

It will impact your ability to stay alert in the classroom and will impact your ability on the field or court.

Ensuring that an athlete has a great breakfast to fuel their day involves a combination of planning, education, and practical strategies.

Here are five keys to achieving this:

- **Educate on the Importance of Breakfast:**
  - We have talked about the importance of breakfast for energy, performance, and overall health.
  - You now understand how a nutritious breakfast can impact your training.
  - If you choose NOT to eat breakfast, just know that it will have a negative impact.
- **Planning and Preparation:**
  - Planning breakfast menus in advance to avoid morning indecision.
  - Preparing breakfast items the night before, like overnight oats or yogurt parfaits, can save time in the morning.
  - You can also use quick and nutritious options that require minimal preparation, such as whole-grain toast with peanut butter, protein smoothies, or boiled eggs.
- **Balanced Nutrition:**
  - We want all 3 macronutrients to be included in breakfast:
    - Carbohydrates for immediate energy and building glycogen
    - Proteins for muscle repair and growth
    - Healthy fats for sustained energy and brain function

- We want a variety of foods that will provide essential vitamins and minerals.
  - Foods like:
    - Whole grains
    - Dairy or dairy alternatives
    - Lean proteins
    - Fruits
    - Nuts
- **Portability for On-the-Go Eating:**
  - For athletes who have early training sessions or who are not morning eaters, you can create portable or on-the-go breakfasts.
  - Foods like:
    - **Homemade Breakfast Burritos:**
      - Fill whole wheat tortillas with scrambled eggs, black beans, cheese, and salsa.
      - These can be made in advance, wrapped in foil or plastic wrap, and reheated in the morning.
      - They're a great source of protein, fiber, and complex carbs.
    - **Peanut Butter and Banana Sandwiches:**
      - Use whole-grain bread to make sandwiches with peanut butter and sliced bananas.
      - This combination provides good fats, protein, and carbohydrates.
      - These sandwiches are easy to eat on the way to school or practice.

- **Overnight Oats in a Jar:**
  - Mix rolled oats with milk or a milk alternative, yogurt, and your choice of sweeteners and toppings like fruits, nuts, or seeds.
  - Prepare them in portable jars or containers.
  - Overnight oats offer a balanced meal with complex carbs, protein, and healthy fats.
- **Homemade Granola Bars or Energy Balls:**
  - Mix oats, nuts, seeds, dried fruit, and honey or peanut butter, and press the mixture into bars or roll into balls.
  - These can be stored in the fridge and grabbed on the go.
  - They're a great source of energy and easy to customize based on preferences and dietary needs.
- **Taste and Personal Preference:**
  - Athletes, choose breakfast foods that you enjoy.
  - A nutritious breakfast is only effective if it's eaten, so taste and personal preference are important.
  - Include a variety of options and encourage athletes to try new foods to keep breakfast interesting and enjoyable.

Breakfast will not only fuel performance on the field or court, but it will also fuel athletes in the classroom.

If an athlete struggles in the morning, that is more reason to eat breakfast.

Paying attention in class is much easier when they have the nutrients in their body to fuel them and regulate hormones and blood sugar.

Our brain consumes 70% of the glucose from our food, meaning carbohydrates fuel our ability to think and reason.

So breakfast in the morning is HIGHLY RECOMMENDED!

Breakfast Options

One of the biggest challenges for teenage athletes is figuring out what to eat.

Cereal is a go-to, but alone, cereal doesn't provide all the macronutrients necessary to fuel our day.

Our goal is to have all three macronutrients at breakfast.

Here are some options to help your athlete fuel up for the day to maximize their performance in the classroom and on the field or court.

- *Peanut Butter Banana Overnight Oats*
  - Protein: 25g
  - Carbs: 45g
  - Fat: 18g
    - Ingredients:
      - ½ cup rolled oats
      - ¾ cup almond milk
      - 2 tbsp peanut butter
      - 1 scoop protein powder (vanilla or unflavored)
      - 1 medium banana, sliced Instructions:
      - Combine rolled oats, almond milk, protein powder, & peanut butter in a jar.
      - Mix well, then add the banana slices on top.
      - Close the jar and refrigerate overnight.
- *Berry Almond Overnight Oats*
  - Protein: 27g

- Carbs: 42g
- Fat: 19g
  - Ingredients:
    - ½ cup rolled oats
    - ¾ cup Greek yogurt
    - ¼ cup mixed berries (e.g., blueberries, strawberries)
    - 2 tbsp almond butter
    - 1 tbsp chia seeds Instructions:
    - Mix all ingredients in a jar.
    - Close the jar and refrigerate overnight.

- **Chocolate Chia Overnight Oats**
  - Protein: 26g
  - Carbs: 50g
  - Fat: 20g
    - Ingredients:
      - ½ cup rolled oats
      - 1 cup almond milk
      - 1 tbsp cocoa powder
      - 1 scoop chocolate protein powder
      - 2 tbsp chia seeds Instructions:
      - Combine all ingredients in a jar.
      - Mix well and refrigerate overnight.

- **Spinach and Feta Omelette**
  - Protein: 28g
  - Carbs: 10g
  - Fat: 19g (Add whole grain toast or fruit to increase carbs)
    - Ingredients:
      - 3 large eggs
      - 1/4 cup feta cheese
      - 1 cup spinach, sautéed

- 1 tbsp olive oil Instructions:
- Heat olive oil in a skillet.
- Add spinach and sauté until wilted.
- In a bowl, whisk eggs and pour over spinach.
- Add feta cheese on top and cook until eggs are set, then fold in half.

- *Egg Muffins with Veggies and Cheese*
  - Protein: 27g (for 3 muffins)
  - Carbs: 15g (Add a side of fruits or toast to meet carb requirements)
  - Fat: 18g
    - Ingredients:
      - 6 large eggs
      - ½ cup diced bell peppers
      - ¼ cup diced onions
      - ½ cup shredded cheddar cheese
      - Salt and pepper to taste Instructions:
      - Preheat the oven to 375°F (190°C).
      - Whisk eggs and mix in the veggies and cheese.
      - Pour the mixture into a muffin tin and bake for 20-25 minutes.

- *Scrambled Eggs with Avocado and Salsa*
  - Protein: 26g
  - Carbs: 20g
  - Fat: 20g
    - Ingredients:
      - 3 large eggs
      - 1 medium avocado, sliced
      - ¼ cup salsa Instructions:

- Scramble eggs in a skillet.
- Serve with avocado slices and top with salsa.

- *Breakfast Burrito*
  - Protein: 30g
  - Carbs: 45g
  - Fat: 20g
    - Ingredients:
      - 2 large eggs, scrambled
      - 1 whole wheat tortilla
      - ¼ cup black beans
      - 2 tbsp salsa
      - ¼ cup shredded cheese Instructions:
      - Place the scrambled eggs, beans, salsa, and cheese in the center of the tortilla.
      - Roll it up and enjoy!

- *Greek Yogurt Parfait*
  - Protein: 25g
  - Carbs: 50g
  - Fat: 17g
    - Ingredients:
      - 1 cup Greek yogurt
      - ½ cup granola
      - ½ cup mixed berries Instructions:
      - Layer yogurt, granola, and berries in a glass or bowl.

- *Quinoa Breakfast Bowl*
  - Protein: 28g
  - Carbs: 50g
  - Fat: 18g
    - Ingredients:

- 1 cup cooked quinoa
- ½ cup Greek yogurt
- 1 tbsp honey
- ¼ cup almonds, chopped
- ½ cup mixed fruit (like berries or banana slices) Instructions:
- Mix quinoa and Greek yogurt in a bowl.
- Top with honey, chopped almonds, and fruit.

- *Peanut Butter and Banana Smoothie*
  - Protein: 30g
  - Carbs: 50g
  - Fat: 20g
    - Ingredients:
      - 1 medium banana
      - 2 tbsp peanut butter
      - 1 scoop protein powder
      - 1 cup almond milk
      - 1 tbsp chia seeds Instructions:
      - Blend all ingredients in a blender until smooth.

- *Tropical Protein Smoothie*
  - Protein: 30g
  - Carbs: 45g
  - Fat: 15g
    - Ingredients:
      - 1 cup unsweetened almond milk (or any milk of your choice)
      - 1 scoop vanilla protein powder
      - 1/2 cup frozen mango chunks
      - 1/2 cup frozen pineapple chunks

- 1/4 cup unsweetened shredded coconut
- 1 tbsp chia seeds
- 1 tbsp flaxseed (optional for added nutrients)
- Ice cubes (optional, for added thickness)
- Instructions:
- Add all ingredients to a blender.
- Blend until smooth and creamy.
- If the consistency is too thick or too thin for your preference, adjust by adding more almond milk or ice.

- *Berry Blast Protein Smoothie*
  - Protein: 28g
  - Carbs: 40g
  - Fat: 15g
    - Ingredients:
      - 1 cup unsweetened almond milk (or any milk of your choice)
      - 1 scoop vanilla or berry-flavored protein powder
      - 1/2 cup frozen blueberries
      - 1/2 cup frozen raspberries
      - 1/2 cup frozen strawberries
      - 1 tbsp almond butter (or peanut butter)
      - 1 tbsp chia seeds
      - Ice cubes (optional, for added thickness)
      - Instructions:
      - Add all ingredients to a blender.
      - Blend until smooth and creamy.
      - Again, if the consistency is not to your liking, adjust with almond milk or ice.

Breakfast is ESSENTIAL for athletes.

These strategies are for our everyday life.

There may be some different breakfast strategies for traveling and tournament days.

We will talk about that below.

Athletes, just know this.

Breakfast is one of the differentiators for those that want to play at a high level.

Start off the day right by fueling your body for success.

EAT BREAKFAST!

CHAPTER 9

LUNCH - THE MIDDAY POWER UP

"Lunch is a midday recharge. It is important to fuel the rest of your day."

- Justin Kegley

Lunch is the midday day fuel up.

It is an integral part of the day to fuel performance in the classroom for the afternoon.

Lunch is also imperative to nourish athletes for practices or games, especially those that occur right after school.

When you're training hard, every meal counts and lunch is a big one.

Let's dive into why certain nutrients are essential and how young athletes can get them without resorting to the school vending machine or settling for a packaged snack.

The ideal lunch includes all three macronutrients:

- Protein
- Carbohydrates
- Fat

Lunch is another meal that requires planning and preparation.

Packing your lunch at home is always the best way to get the macro and micro nutrients you need to fuel the rest of your day.

If your school has great options for lunch, then eating at school can be an option.

Most of the time though, this is not the case and packing your food will be important.

Athletes also need to know that eating food out of the vending machine or a significant amount of prepackaged meals will prevent them from fueling their bodies appropriately.

Plus, it can get costly.

Let's talk about packing your lunch and how you can make choices that will taste great and fuel your performance.

Creating the Ideal Athlete's Lunch – Practical and Portable:

- **Sandwich Supreme:**
    - Whole grain bread offers carbs and fiber, while lean meats like turkey or chicken provide protein.
    - Add sliced avocado for healthy fats, and stack it with veggies for added nutrients.
    - Easy to wrap and go!
- **Power-Packed Salad Bowl:**
    - Dark leafy greens are your base.
    - Add grilled chicken for protein, cherry tomatoes, and cucumber slices, and sprinkle with seeds or chopped nuts.
    - Use a squeeze of lemon and olive oil for flavor.
    - Pack it in a leak-proof container, and it's ready to go!
- **Wrap It Up:**
    - Whole grain or spinach wraps filled with veggies, lean meats, or even a bit of cheese can be delicious and nourishing.
    - They're also easy to hold and eat.
- **Snack Wisely:**
    - Instead of raiding vending machines, bring from home some Greek yogurt topped with fruits or make a trail

mix with nuts, seeds, and a few chocolate chips for a treat.
  - Carrot sticks with hummus or apple slices with peanut butter are also excellent options.

Things to Remember:

- **Avoiding Junk:**
  - It's important to skip foods high in refined sugars, excessive fats, and artificial additives.
  - They might offer a quick energy spike, but it's short-lived and followed by a crash.
  - Just because others are doing it doesn't mean you should.
  - Fuel yourself like a champion.
- **Packaged Foods:**
  - Reduce your dependence on them.
  - Not all are bad, but many contain hidden sugars, unhealthy fats, and preservatives.
  - If you must, look for those with short ingredient lists.
- **Stay Hydrated:**
  - Always have a water bottle on hand.
  - Proper hydration is essential for muscle function and recovery.

With some planning and a focus on whole, unprocessed foods, high school athletes can enjoy lunches that fuel their performance and keep them alert in the classroom.

Here are 10 lunch recipes that can help athletes prepare their meals in advance and maximize their energy and performance in the classroom and on the field or court.

- *Chicken Pesto Wrap*
  - 3 oz. grilled chicken strips

- 1 large whole-wheat tortilla
- 2 tbsp. pesto sauce
- Spinach or lettuce
- Sliced tomatoes
  - Side Options:
    - Baby carrots
    - Small apple
    - Handful of pretzels

- *Mediterranean Veggie Sandwich*
  - 2 slices whole grain bread
  - 3 tbsp. hummus
  - Sliced cucumbers
  - Sliced red onions
  - Sliced tomatoes
  - Feta cheese crumbles
    - Sides:
      - Bell pepper strips
      - Grapes
      - Baked chips.

- *Turkey & Swiss on Rye*
  - 2 slices rye bread
  - 3 oz. turkey breast slices
  - 1 slice Swiss cheese
  - Lettuce and tomatoes
  - 1 tbsp. Dijon mustard
    - Sides:
      - Celery sticks
      - Banana
      - Handful of pretzels.

- *BBQ Beef Wrap*
  - 3 oz. roast beef slices

- 1 large whole wheat tortilla
- 2 tbsp. BBQ sauce
- Sliced red onions
- Lettuce
    - Sides:
        - Cucumber slices,
        - Orange
        - Baked chips.
- *Italian Deli Wrap*
    - 1 large whole wheat tortilla
    - 1 oz. salami, 1 oz. ham, 1 oz. provolone cheese
    - Sliced olives
    - Sliced tomatoes
    - 1 tbsp. Italian dressing
        - Sides:
            - Broccoli florets
            - Pear
            - Baked chips
- *BLT Sandwich*
    - 2 slices whole grain bread
    - 3 slices cooked bacon
    - Lettuce
    - Tomato slices
    - 1 tbsp. mayo
        - Sides:
            - Carrot sticks
            - Mixed fruit
            - Pretzels
- *Ranch Chicken Wrap*
    - 3 oz. grilled chicken strips
    - 1 large whole wheat tortilla

- 2 tbsp. ranch dressing
- Sliced cucumbers
- Lettuce
  - Sides:
    - Snap peas
    - Apple,
    - Baked chips
- *Ham & Honey Mustard Sandwich*
  - 2 slices whole grain bread
  - 3 oz. ham slices
  - 2 tbsp. honey mustard
  - Lettuce and tomatoes
    - Sides:
      - Cauliflower florets
      - Banana
      - Handful of pretzels

Lunch is the opportunity to fuel the rest of your day.

Do not skip over this important meal that can help you prepare for the afternoon that lies ahead.

Take the time to set up your meals in advance so you

CHAPTER 10

DINNER - SETTING THE STAGE FOR TOMORROW'S SUCCESS

"Nutrition is so important. It can't be stressed enough.

- Dwayne Johnson

Are we eating at 4 pm or 9 pm?

If you are a family with athletes, this is a REAL question!

Dinner is challenging in a different way than lunch or breakfast.

The goal used to be to eat dinner together all around a table every night.

Now, we are running at such a fast pace that makes it almost impossible.

Families of athletes have to adapt, often going in different directions at night.

This means that sitting down together is difficult, if not impossible most days of the week.

The second challenge is eating out.

We have generally accepted eating fast food or quick order service often.

This is a problem.

Parents spend their hard earned time and money trying to provide for all the training, practice and games.

Yet, we have accepted the fact that we should eat out because it's convenient.

I know this is a challenge, but let's be honest, buying all the 1:1 coaching, training and getting on the right travel team doesn't mean anything if an athlete is fueling with garbage.

Athletes will never achieve their maximum performance fueling with crap.

In addition to that, this is a pattern of behavior that will lead to more obesity over time.

I don't mean to put all this on parents either, but the habits our kids have is directly related to what we allow.

In terms of eating at dinner, we want another meal with ALL the macronutrients in it.

- Protein
- Carbohydrates
- Fat

One question we often get is whether they should eat late or right before they go to bed.

Yes.

If an athlete eats a meal that is part of their daily nutrition plan, then they should eat late.

Getting appropriate nutrients into your system is a priority for high performance and scientifically, it doesn't matter about nutrient timing if it is within their plan.

The best option for an athlete is to eat dinner at home at the table, preferably with the rest of the family.

This allows for a connection and a break from our fast-paced world.

If this is not an option, then preparation will be the key.

Eating out at fast food restaurants consistently makes nutrition HARD!

There are too many uncontrolled variables.

Eating fast food poses several health risks for high school athletes, and many of these risks stem from uncontrolled variables inherent in fast food. Here are five such variables:

- **High Caloric Density:**
  - Fast food is often calorie-dense, providing lots of calories in small amounts of food.
  - This can lead to overeating.
- **Excessive Sodium Content:**
  - Fast food tends to be very high in sodium.
  - This leads to:
    - Excessive water retention
    - High blood pressure
    - High sodium intake can also affect an athlete's hydration status, which is crucial for performance.
- **Low Nutritional Quality:**
  - Fast food often lacks essential nutrients like vitamins, minerals, and fiber.
  - Many fast food items are high in unhealthy fats.
  - Athletes require a diet rich in these nutrients for energy, recovery, muscle repair, and overall health.
  - The lack of nutrients in fast food makes it a poor dietary choice for athletes.
- **High Sugar Content:**
  - Fast food often contains high amounts of added sugars.
    - Beverages
    - Desserts
  - Excessive sugar intake can lead to:
    - Energy spikes and crashes.
    - Affect insulin sensitivity.
    - Contribute to weight gain.

These uncontrolled variables make fast food an unhealthy choice for high school athletes, who need balanced, nutrient-rich diets to perform at their best.

There are going to be times when an athlete is going to have to eat fast food.

This is particularly the case for tournaments and road games.

But, during your normal routine, the goal should be to eat home-cooked meals as much as possible, even if pre-packaged and warmed up on the road.

Does this take planning and effort, yes!

But, if you want to be a high-performance athlete, work will be required.

This also teaches an athlete the importance of preparing food in advance and reducing their dependence on fast-food restaurants.

Learning to prepare food will help athletes learn life skills and create opportunities for parents and athletes to spend quality time together.

In addition to the health benefits of eating at home, there is a family quality time that is desperately needed.

Eating at home together is good for the family.

If it can be done, do it.

Dinner at home is not always an option though.

So, preparing food together with your athlete is an opportunity.

Meal prepping is not glamorous, but it is a great way to stay on track.

It can either be a chore that "has to be done," or it can be a choice that allows for time together in a hurried world.

This is a chance to explore new foods, teach an athlete how to cook and care for themselves more and master great habits that will serve them as adults.

If you are looking for dinner options, here are some great recipes:

Grilled Chicken Salad with Quinoa

- Chicken: Season with salt, pepper, and any preferred herbs.
- Grill for 6-8 minutes each side or until internal temperature reaches 165°F (74°C).
- Quinoa: Rinse, then cook in boiling water (1 part quinoa to 2 parts water) for 15 minutes or until translucent.
- Dressing: Mix olive oil, balsamic vinegar, salt, and pepper.

Stir-fry Beef with Brown Rice

- Beef: In a hot pan with sesame oil, stir fry beef until browned.
- Add sliced veggies and sauté until tender.
- Season with soy sauce or tamari.
- Brown Rice: Cook according to package instructions.

Salmon Fillet with Sweet Potato

- Salmon: Season with salt, pepper, and lemon slices.
- Bake at 400°F (204°C) for 12-15 minutes.
- Sweet Potato: Pierce with a fork and bake at 400°F (204°C) for 45 minutes or until soft.

Turkey & Vegetable Pasta

- Turkey: In a pan with olive oil, cook ground turkey until browned.
- Pasta: Boil whole wheat spaghetti as per package instructions.
- Sauté veggies in garlic and olive oil until tender.
- Combine with cooked pasta and turkey.
- Garnish with herbs.

Pork Tenderloin with Lentils

- Pork: Season as desired and grill or oven-roast at 400°F (204°C) for 20-25 minutes or until internal temp reaches 145°F (63°C).
- Allow to rest before slicing.
- Lentils: Rinse and cook in boiling water (1 part lentils to 2 parts water) until tender.

Shrimp Tacos with Whole Grain Tortillas

- Shrimp: Season and grill for 2-3 minutes each side.
- Warm tortillas in a dry pan for 30 seconds on each side.
- Assembly: Place shrimp in tortillas and add toppings.

Steak with Cauliflower Mash and Greens

- Steak: Season steak and grill to the desired doneness.
- Cauliflower Mash: Steam cauliflower until tender.
- Mash with garlic, olive oil, salt, and pepper until smooth.
- Greens: Sauté spinach and mushrooms in olive oil until wilted.

Tuna Salad Stuffed Bell Peppers

- Tuna Salad: Mix drained tuna, Greek yogurt, mustard, and celery.
- Bell Peppers: Halve and remove seeds.
- Stuff with tuna mix.
- For a tender pepper, serve raw or bake at 375°F (190°C) for 20 minutes.

Lamb Chops with Roasted Vegetables

- Lamb Chops: Season and grill to the desired doneness.
- Veggies: Toss veggies in olive oil, salt, pepper, and rosemary.
- Roast at 400°F (204°C) for 20-25 minutes.

Chicken & Bean Burrito Bowl

- Chicken: Season and grill until internal temperature reaches 165°F (74°C).

- Beans & Rice: Cook separately according to package instructions.
- Veggies: Sauté bell peppers and onions in coconut oil until tender.

Eating Late at Night

One frequently asked question is, "What about eating late at night."

If the food is part of the plan, go ahead.

If it's not, then be cautious.

Eating late at night is not a great habit for life.

It can impact your sleep duration and your REM sleep cycle.

As we age, it doesn't help us maintain a healthy lifestyle.

For athletes, eating late works because we need to ensure they are getting enough calories in their system to help them recover and refuel.

If they have a practice that runs later at night, they will need to eat afterwards.

Eating late can be a strategy for those looking to increase weight.

The goal would be to eat and at least give yourself 30-60 minutes before going to bed.

Ideally, it would be 2-3 hours.

These meals should focus on protein, fat, complex carbohydrates, and less simple carbohydrates.

The challenge will be ensuring that food is prepared in advance and athletes are not just rummaging the pantry.

At this point in the day, we especially want athletes to choose whole foods over prepackaged snacks.

Pantry eating is one area that can harm athletes.

One rule that works for our family is to have two things from the pantry for the day.

That means that anything in the fridge is fair game, but we limit the amount of processed foods we eat by reducing the amount of packaged snacks consumed from the pantry.

When eating late at night, it's easy to go to the pantry.

So limit the opportunity to go there with simple rules that will help athletes not only eat better now but also help them learn great life habits.

CHAPTER 11

| FUELING BEFORE AND AFTER ACTIVITY.

"Food is your body's fuel. Without fuel, your body wants to shut down."

- Ken Hill

Pre and Post workout nutrition is crucial for high performance.

{Side note: workout in this context accounts for practices, games, workouts, or moderate to high-intensity training.}

There is one big key to eating before and after practice, training or games.

We want to limit the amount of fats that we consume.

We aim to get protein and carbohydrates into our system with little fats.

The reason why is because fats slow digestion.

Before and after practices, training, or games, we want to restore energy and begin the muscle repair process as soon as possible.

The exception to this would be in a tournament or multiple-game scenario. *{More on this later}*

Pre-Workout Nutrition

This can look different based on the practice, training, or game time.

If the practice, training, or game is after school, this looks like a quick snack that can help regulate blood sugar and provide energy before playing.

This doesn't need to be a large snack.

Just enough to help replenish some energy stores and boost you before you play.

Typically, this would have a bit of protein (15-25 g) and more carbohydrates (30-60 g).

The size of the snack depends on your ability to tolerate food before playing and your size.

If the practice, training, or game is not immediately after school, maybe 6-8 p.m., then eating dinner would be the best option.

Again, this depends on the athlete's ability to tolerate food before playing and their size.

We want food in our system at least 1 hour before playing.

Pre-Workout Options

Non-Fat Greek Yogurt & Honey
- 1 cup nonfat Greek yogurt (approx. 15g protein)
- 2 tablespoons honey (approx. 34g carbs)

Egg White Omelette & Toast
- 1 cup egg whites (approx. 25g protein)
- 2 slices of white bread toasted (approx. 30g carbs)
- Optional: add a splash of ketchup or hot sauce for flavor

Tuna (in water) on White Bread
- 1 can of tuna in water, drained (approx. 20g protein)
- 2 slices of white bread (approx. 30g carbs)

Protein Smoothie
- 1 scoop of protein powder (approx. 20g protein, varies by brand)
- 1 medium ripe banana (approx. 27g carbs)
- Water to blend

Turkey Sandwich
- 90g lean turkey slices (approx. 15g protein)

- 2 slices of white bread (approx. 30g carbs)
- Optional: a small amount of non-fat mayo for moisture

Low-Fat Cottage Cheese & Canned Pineapple

- 1 cup low-fat cottage cheese (approx. 15g protein)
- 1/2 cup canned pineapple in juice (not syrup) (approx. 15g carbs)
- 1 tablespoon honey (approx. 17g carbs)

White Pasta with Chicken

- 90g grilled chicken pieces (approx. 20g protein)
- 1 cup cooked white pasta (approx. 43g carbs)
- Drizzle with a small amount of low-sodium soy sauce

Egg White Wrap

- 1 cup egg whites (approx. 25g protein)
- 1 white tortilla wrap (approx. 30g carbs, check label as it can vary)
- Optional: a splash of hot sauce for flavor

Whey Protein Shake & Pretzels

- 1 scoop of whey protein powder mixed with water (approx. 20g protein, varies by brand)
- 1 serving of pretzels (check label, approx. 30-40g carbs depending on serving size)

Grilled Chicken & White Rice

- 90g grilled chicken breast (approx. 20g protein)
- 1/2 cup cooked white rice (approx. 22g carbs)
- Drizzle with lemon juice or a splash of low-sodium soy sauce for flavor

Post-Workout Nutrition

Post-workout meals are essential for replenishing muscle glycogen and to stimulate muscle protein synthesis following training.

After practice, game, or training, we want to get food into our system as soon as possible.

The goal is to eat within the first 30-60 minutes.

This will start the repairing and refueling process.

Refueling can be challenging for some as difficult training sessions or games can make it hard to eat right away.

Don't force your athlete to eat immediately if they can't tolerate it.

We don't want to make them sick.

But, we do want to begin the recovery process as soon as possible.

Ideally, the post-workout meal consists of protein and carbohydrates with limited fats.

One excellent option post-workout is *low fat chocolate milk*.

Regular chocolate milk.

It has protein and carbohydrates.

It will also help with our hydration, which is a GREAT option.

Another option that is quick and easy is a protein shake with a banana or other fruit.

Also, it doesn't have to be a shake or chocolate milk; it can be whole food.

The goal is to get something into your system ASAP to start the repair process.

Ideally, this is prepared in advance so you can consume it at the facility or while you are leaving!

Consumption of carbs and protein in post-workout nutrition looks like a 2:1 or 3:1 carbohydrate-to-protein ratio.

Your goal in this scenario is to consume around 20-25 g of protein and 40-75 g of carbohydrates.

The amount of carbs can vary depending on the workout's intensity or the athlete's size.

Post-Workout Options

Chocolate Milk Shake

- 2 cups of low-fat chocolate milk (16 g protein, 52 g carbs).

Whey Protein Smoothie

- 1 scoop of whey protein (varies, typically around 25 g protein).
- 1 large banana (30 g carbs).
- 1 cup of milk (around 12 g carbs).
- Blend all ingredients.

Rice & Chicken Bowl

- 1 cup of cooked white rice (45 g carbs, 4 g protein).
- 4 oz of skinless grilled chicken breast (about 25 g protein).
- Optional: A splash of soy sauce or low-sodium teriyaki for flavor.

Protein Pancakes

- Use a pre-made protein pancake mix (many are available that provide around 20 g protein and 50-60 g carbs per serving).
- Top with 1 tablespoon of maple syrup or honey for the additional carbs.

Quinoa & Tuna Salad

- 1 cup of cooked quinoa (39 g carbs, 8 g protein).
- 4 oz of canned tuna in water (around 25 g protein).
- Season with lemon juice and herbs for flavor.

Adjust the portion sizes as needed to meet the macronutrient goals for your athlete.

Opt for quick cooking or instant rice and quinoa to speed up preparation.

These meals are designed to give the body the necessary nutrients post-workout quickly. The combination of fast-digesting carbs and protein supports muscle recovery and growth.

CHAPTER 12

EATING ON THE ROAD - STRATEGIES FOR TOURNAMENTS

"Self-discipline is the ability to make yourself do what you should do when you should do it, whether you feel like it or not."

- Elbert Hubbard

Youth sports are filled with travel tournaments.

Playing multiple games in one day or playing games over the course of a weekend is the norm..

Eating on the road or in-between games can be a real challenge.

Really, the objective is to control the chaos.

Prepare in advance as much as possible because we don't know when we'll be playing.

This chapter will have lots of what if's, but I will work to provide you with multiple options to cover a multitude of schedules.

The goal for these tournaments is to be prepared and help our athletes recover as fast as possible from one game to the next.

Sometimes the tournaments are in an area that has great options for food and other times they are not.

One of the biggest downfalls of travel tournaments for athletes and parents is the lack of preparation.

Lots of pizza, sub sandwiches, snacks, sugar and more.

This type of food is not only not healthy in the long term, but it is counter to the goal of nutrition for sports, which is to fuel performance.

We are so busy playing and watching the games that we don't take a moment to think about what we are going to eat until we are hungry, then we need food NOW!

I certainly don't expect perfection, but limiting the amount of sugar and processed food is going to be important.

First off, if you are a travel family, then these tournaments are happening regularly.

This means that it is not a vacation every weekend where you can just eat junk and get away with it.

It will sabotage your performance on the field or court as well as create awful habits for life.

It also depends on the type of sport the athlete is playing.

Sports that are more aerobic like soccer, field hockey and endurance running events are going to require both carbohydrates and fats to fuel performance.

Sports that are more Anaerobic, like basketball, volleyball, baseball, softball, wrestling, swimming, track and field, ice hockey utilize muscle glycogen for performance for quick, intense bursts of energy.

Energy will come more from carbohydrates than fat.

All sports will need protein in appropriate amounts to repair muscles.

Planning is going to be important.

It takes a little bit of time, but that can help prevent poor fueling, upset stomachs and managing hormones that control emotions.

Here are some questions to ask in advance of a tournament.

- How far away from home are you?
- Can you take food with you?
- Can you pack a cooler bag or rolling cooler?

- Are you staying in a hotel or a short-term rental home?
- Do you have access to a refrigerator?
- Do you have access to a kitchen?
- Will you be cooking any meals?
- Are you staying in a hotel with breakfast included?
- If yes, is the breakfast worth eating?
    - Prepackaged foods v. Continental Breakfast?
    - If not, where will you eat?
- How much time will it take to get to the venue?
- Do you have access to a grocery store?

Preparation will prevent you from making quick decisions that often end in regret.

The priority is to make sure the athlete is fueled before the game, recovers in between games on the same day, and is prepared to play their best for the next day.

Also, tournaments generally require early morning games.

This creates a challenge for many athletes as they don't want to eat before a game that starts early.

It may upset their stomach or they just don't want to wake up any earlier than they have to.

For this type of athlete, eating a full meal the night before will be necessary.

The food they eat the 12-24 hours before their game will be crucial to providing the energy they need.

For a full meal, we are looking for protein, carbohydrates, and fat..

Something that will provide the protein they need to repair their muscles as well as the carbohydrates and fat needed to restore their energy systems for the next day.

Dinner after a long day of playing is going to be CRUCIAL!

Less pizza and fast food, more complete sit down meals that are higher quality

That is a priority for the night before a tournament and all nights that have a game the following day.

Of course, the timing of games matters.

If athletes are playing late in the evening, preparation will be necessary.

If a late night is followed by an early morning, then preparation is even more critical.

Every person is different, and schedules can create challenges.

On the morning of a game, our real goal is to regulate blood sugar and provide some carbohydrates to ensure appropriate energy stores.

If athletes are playing before 9 a.m., it can be hard to get a solid meal in without feeling like they have food in their stomachs.

So, breakfast can be simple and small.

Oatmeal and Milk:
- 1/2 cup cooked oatmeal
- A small handful of berries
- 1 Cup of Milk

Greek Yogurt Parfait:
- 3/4 cup non-fat Greek yogurt
- 1/3 cup granola
- 1/2 banana, sliced

Whole Grain Toast with Cottage Cheese:
- 2 slices of whole grain toast
- 1/2 cup low-fat cottage cheese
- Drizzle of honey and sprinkle of cinnamon

Protein Pancakes:
- Prepare using a protein-packed pancake mix (like Kodiak Cakes) as per instructions

- Top with a drizzle of sugar-free syrup and a handful of berries

Protein Bar:
- Many protein bars on the market fit within this criteria.
- Look for ones with whole ingredients like:
  - RXBAR
  - KIND Protein
  - Or Barebells Protein bars.

Egg White Scramble with Whole Grain Toast:
- Scramble 1 cup of egg whites with veggies like spinach and tomatoes
- Serve with 1 slice of whole grain toast

Smoothie Bowl:
- Blend 1 scoop protein powder, 1/2 banana, 1/4 cup oats, and enough almond milk to reach desired consistency
- Top with a small amount of granola and berries

Quinoa Breakfast Bowl:
- 1/2 cup cooked quinoa
- 1/4 cup non-fat Greek yogurt
- 1/2 banana, sliced
- Drizzle of honey and sprinkle of chia seeds

Peanut butter and Jelly on a Bagel:
- 1 Serving of peanut butter
- 1-2 Servings of jelly
- Spread on a bagel

Fruit with Milk
- Pick a Fruit
  - Banana
  - Apple
  - Orange
  - Strawberries

- Blueberries
- 1 Cup of milk

These are all great options to get something in their system that isn't as heavy as a full meal.

It doesn't have to be complicated.

Just make sure to get a little something into their stomach before a game, as long as it doesn't make them sick or nauseous.

Having your athlete decide the night before what they will eat is one way to remove the battle in the morning.

In Between Games

There are two options here.

- Back-to-Back Games
- Games with long delays in between

Back-to-Back Games

If an athlete is playing back-to-back games, the most important thing is to rehydrate with an electrolyte drink higher in sodium, especially if the playing conditions are at a higher temperature.

We want something that has more than 250 mg of sodium while also including potassium.

LMNT, Gatorade or Liquid IV will fulfill this requirement.

You should be consuming 20-24 ounces per pound of bodyweight lost per game.

If your athlete is playing significant minutes, they need to at least drink 40-48 ounces of water or electrolyte drink following a game.

If you are not playing significant minutes, or have a less taxing sport, then 20-24 ounces of water will suffice.

Once hydration has been taken care of, then we can talk about food.

Games with quick turnaround times can be challenging.

Typically, there isn't much time, so quick snacks here can be important.

Fruit, granola bars, and peanut butter and jelly sandwiches can all be great options.

We are looking to replace energy stores quickly.

Athletes should eat to tolerance, as we don't want to make them sick during the next game.

Certainly! Here are five quick snack ideas for athletes that are each under 300 calories, ideal for a quick energy boost between games:

Greek Yogurt with Honey and Almonds:
- One small container of nonfat Greek yogurt (about 100 calories).
- A drizzle of honey (1 teaspoon, about 20 calories).
- A sprinkle of sliced almonds (1 tablespoon, about 40 calories).
- This snack provides protein from the yogurt, a quick energy boost from the honey, and healthy fats from the almonds.

Apple Slices with Peanut Butter:
- One medium apple, sliced (about 95 calories).
- One tablespoon of peanut butter (about 95 calories).
- This combination offers a good mix of carbohydrates, protein, and healthy fats.

Mixed Berries and Cottage Cheese:
- One-half cup of low-fat cottage cheese (about 90 calories).
- One cup of mixed berries like strawberries, blueberries, and raspberries (about 70 calories).
- - The berries provide quick-digesting carbs and antioxidants, while the cottage cheese offers protein.

Whole Grain Crackers with Cheese:

- Four to five whole grain crackers (about 100 calories).
- One stick of low-fat string cheese or a slice of cheese (about 60-80 calories).
- This snack is a good source of carbohydrates and calcium-rich protein.

Turkey Avocado Sandwich:
- Ingredients:
    - 2 slices of whole grain bread.
    - 3-4 slices of turkey breast (low sodium).
    - 2 slices of tomato.
    - 2 leaves of romaine lettuce.
    - 2 thin slices of avocado.
    - Mustard or a light spread of mayonnaise (optional).
- Side:
    - A small bag (about 1 oz) of baked vegetable chips.

Chicken Salad Sandwich
- Ingredients:
    - 2 slices of whole wheat bread.
    - ½ cup of cooked, shredded chicken breast.
    - 1 tablespoon of Greek yogurt (or light mayonnaise).
    - 1 teaspoon of Dijon mustard.
    - A handful of mixed greens or spinach.
    - Salt and pepper to taste.
- Side:
    - A cup of mixed fresh berries (strawberries, blueberries, raspberries).

Ham, Cheese, and Apple Sandwich
- Ingredients:
    - 2 slices of whole grain bread.

- 3-4 slices of lean ham (preferably low sodium).
  - 1 slice of Swiss cheese or cheddar cheese.
  - Thinly sliced apple (about half an apple).
  - A thin spread of Dijon mustard or honey mustard.
  - A few leaves of fresh spinach or lettuce.
- Side:
  - A small serving of trail mix (a mix of nuts, seeds, and dried fruit, about 1 oz).

These sandwich recipes provide a good balance of carbohydrates, protein, and healthy fats, making them ideal for athletes looking for a nutritious and satisfying meal in between games. The sides add additional nutrients and a bit of variety to the meal.

Games with long delays in between

If the tournament has long delays in between, then the goal should be to get a whole meal in as soon as possible after the first game.

We want to replace energy stores and help the recovery process in between games.

The focus here is to provide more complex carbohydrates rather than sugar.

We want to replenish energy stores with foods that will provide lasting energy.

Simple carbohydrates here would be a mistake as they can cause energy spikes and dips.

Get a whole meal with protein and carbohydrates such as:

- Whole grain rice
- Pasta, potatoes
- Sweet potatoes
- Oatmeal

- Fruits
- Vegetables.

This meal should look like the night-before game meal.

The portions should be larger and provide protein, carbohydrates, and fats.

Going to a restaurant for a sit down meal would be the best option here, unless you have packed meals in advance for this.

Also, this meal should be combined with rest, since we have hours before the next game.

Minimize screen time for athletes on game day, but in particular in between games to be able to maximize focus.

Sample Meal Plans for Tournament Schedules

Example: 8 am game and 1 pm Game

Evening Before:
- Focus on staying well-hydrated the day before the game.
- Follow hydration guidelines in hydration chapter
- Dinner (Night Before):High in complex carbohydrates, moderate protein, low in fat. Examples: Grilled chicken, whole grain pasta, and steamed vegetables.

Day of Tournament Early Morning (6:30 AM)
- Snack: Aim for something light but energy-boosting.
  - Options:
  - Banana with a small peanut butter sandwich
  - Greek yogurt with berries
  - Protein bar.
  - See meals above
- Drink: Water and/or an electrolyte drink.
  - See chart above

Post-First Game (Around 9:30 AM)

- Goal: Replenish energy, provide protein for muscle recovery.
    - Meal: Grilled chicken breast or steak
    - Brown rice or quinoa
    - Mixed vegetables.
- Drink:
    - Water

Mid-Day Meal (11:30 AM - 12:00 PM)

- Meal: Lighter, easily digestible foods to prepare for the next game.
    - Options:
        - Turkey or hummus wrap with whole grain bread
- Drink: Continue with water and maybe a small electrolyte beverage.

Post-Second Game (Around 2:30 PM)

- Goal: Similar to the first post-game meal, focus on recovery.
- Meal:
    - Options:
        - Grilled salmon, sweet potato, and green beans.
- Drink: Water.

Evening Meal (6:00 PM - 7:00 PM)

- Meal: Balanced, focused on protein, carbohydrates and fat
- Recovering from the day of games and preparing for tomorrow's games.
    - Options: Lean steak or chicken,
    - Whole grain pasta or brown rice

- ○ Mix of roasted vegetables.
- Drink: Water.

Example: Back to Back games at 11am & 12 pm

Evening Before:

- Focus on staying well-hydrated the day before the game.
- Follow hydration guidelines in hydration chapter
- Dinner (Night Before):High in complex carbohydrates, moderate protein, low in fat. Examples: Grilled chicken, whole grain pasta, and steamed vegetables.

Day of Tournament Breakfast (8:00 AM)

- Goal: Full breakfast with protein, carbohydrates and fat.
- Athletes will have time to digest this full meal before warmups begin an hour prior to game time, so eat well.l
- Meal: **Egg White Scramble with Whole Grain Toast:**
  - ○ Scramble 1 cup of egg whites with veggies like spinach and tomatoes
  - ○ Serve with 1 slice of whole grain toast
- Drink: Water and/or a glass of milk.

Pre-Game Snack (10:30 AM)

- Snack: Something to provide a quick energy boost.
- Options:
  - ○ A granola bar
  - ○ Piece of fruit like an apple or a banana
  - ○ Small yogurt.
- Drink: Water, stay hydrated but not overly full.

Between Games (11:45 AM)

- Snack: Quick, light, and energy-replenishing.
- Options:
  - ○ Sandwich and Pretzels
  - ○ Piece of Fruit such as banana or oranges
- Drink: Water and electrolyte drink.

110

Post-Games Recovery (1:00 PM)

- Goal: Rehydrate and start muscle recovery.
- Meal: Balanced, focused on protein, carbohydrates and fat
- Recovering games.
    - Options: Lean steak or chicken,
    - Whole grain pasta or brown rice
    - Mix of roasted vegetables.
- Drink: Water.

Mid-Afternoon Meal (4:00 PM)

- Meal: Focus on replenishing energy stores and providing nutrients for recovery.
    - Options:
    - Turkey or veggie wrap with avocado
    - Side of carrot sticks
    - Piece of fruit.
- Drink: Water

Evening Meal (7:00 PM)

- Meal:A balanced, more substantial meal to support recovery and replenish energy stores.
    - Options:
    - Baked chicken
    - Vegetables
    - Quinoa or brown rice.
- Drink: Water, and if desired, a glass of milk or a non-caffeinated beverage.

Night Snack (If Necessary)

- Snack: If hungry before bed, eat something light.
- Options:
    - Bowl of cottage cheese with fruit
    - Slice of whole grain toast with almond butter.

- Drink: Water

Keys to Success

- **Hydration:**
  - Maintain hydration throughout the day with water and electrolyte drinks as needed.
- **Balance:**
  - Meas immediately following games should have a good balance of carbohydrates (for energy), protein (for muscle repair), and fats (for sustained energy).
  - Before games, limit the amount of fats an athlete consumes.
- **Timing:**
  - The goal is to eat approximately every 3 hours to keep energy levels stable.
  - Manage energy with snacks in between games.
- **Portion Control:**
  - Avoid large meals right before games to prevent feeling sluggish or having an upset stomach.
- **Listen to Your Body:**
  - Adjust portion sizes and snack choices based on hunger and energy levels.
  - We need fuel for recovery, but we also don't want to make an athlete sick.

CHAPTER 13

SUPPLEMENTS - SHOULD MY ATHLETE TAKE THEM?

"The ultimate resource is resourcefulness. That's what makes someone successful."

- Tony Robbins

Club and high school sports are competitive.

Athletes are constantly seeking ways to enhance their performance.

In order to get an advantage, some athletes look to the world of supplements to help them achieve peak performance.

Unfortunately, this is short sided thinking for most.

The focus should be on getting your nutrients from whole food sources, rather than from a pill or powder.

There are times when supplements can help, but they should be a SUPPLEMENT (hence the name) to a great diet.

Here is our take on supplements for developing athletes.

Pre-Workouts
- Based on our earlier chapter speaking to hydration, we have already talked about caffeine and how we DO NOT recommend it for anyone under 18.
- Pre-workouts deserve a specific spot in supplements though because I want to drive the point home that these are NOT recommended.
- Whether in powder form or in a can, they contain excessive amounts of caffeine, amino acids, vitamins,

and sometimes herbs or other substances claiming to boost energy and athletic performance.

- Pre-workouts promise intensity increases during training, so they can be tempting.
- There are significant risks though.

High Caffeine Content:

- Many pre-workout supplements contain high levels of caffeine.
- Excessive caffeine intake can lead to side effects such as
  - Increased heart rate
  - High blood pressure
  - Anxiety
  - Sleep Disruption
  - Digestive issues
- For high school athletes, whose bodies are still developing, large amounts of caffeine are a problem.

Safety and Regulation:

- The supplement industry is not regulated.
- This means pre-workout supplements' safety, quality, and efficacy can vary significantly between products.
- They may also contain harmful ingredients or contaminants not listed on the label.

Risk of Dependency:

- There's a risk of developing a psychological or physical dependency on these supplements to perform
- This is unhealthy for young athletes both mentally and physically.

Hiding Fatigue:

- Pre-workouts mask the feelings of tiredness, leading athletes to push beyond safe limits and increasing the risk of injury.

Nutritional Imbalance:

- Refrain from focusing on pre-workout supplements to avoid neglecting important aspects of nutrition, such as eating a good pre-activity meal that provides sustained energy.

Our Stance on Caffeine:

- To reiterate, given the potential risks of large amounts of caffeine, I recommend avoiding caffeine supplements for high school athletes.
- The focus should instead be on achieving energy and performance boosts through a well-balanced diet, adequate sleep, and proper hydration.

Multivitamins

- Multivitamins are one of a few supplements that I would recommend to athletes.
- It is hard to get everything you need out of your food, even if you eat extremely well!
- Multivitamins can fill nutritional gaps in an athlete's diet, especially if they have dietary restrictions or allergies.
- This ensures that athletes get essential vitamins and minerals necessary for overall health, energy production, and muscle recovery.

Glutamine

- Glutamine is an amino acid that aids in muscle recovery and boosts immune function.
- Athletes undergoing intense training benefit from glutamine because it can reduce muscle soreness and recovery time.
- The body usually produces enough glutamine, and it is also available in many protein-rich foods.

- Adding this supplement is generally unnecessary for high school athletes unless under extreme physical stress or illness.

Creatine
- Creatine is one of the most researched supplements, with over 700 studies!
- It improves strength, increases lean muscle mass, and helps muscles recover more quickly during practice and training.
- This is especially beneficial in sports that require quick bursts of energy like sprinting or weightlifting.
- Creatine for anyone under 16 is not recommended.
- While you can get creatine from food, it is difficult to get the appropriate dose.
- 3-5 g is the daily recommended dose.
- The only ingredient you need is Creatine Monohydrate, nothing else.
- There is no need to buy products that have combinations of products, just Creatine Monohydrate.

Omega-3 Fatty Acids
- This is a supplement that we HIGHLY RECOMMEND for athletes.
- As mentioned before, it is difficult to get all the Omega-3's in our diet, so supplementation makes sense.
- Omega-3 supplements have anti-inflammatory effects and benefits to heart and brain health.
- For high school athletes, Omega-3's may assist in:
  - Recovery by reducing muscle soreness.
  - Improve joint health.
  - Protect the brain.

- The NIH recommends the following dosage for high school athletes:
  - 1.6 g of omega-3's per day for males.
  - 1.1 g of omega-3's per day for females.

Branched-Chain Amino Acids (BCAAs)

- BCAA supplements are unnecessary for anyone that consumes sufficient amounts of high-quality protein sources.
- BCAAs are essential amino acids, particularly leucine, isoleucine, and valine.
- They promote muscle protein synthesis and reduce muscle breakdown, potentially enhancing recovery and adaptation to training.
- BCAA's are essential, meaning we must get them from our diet, but taking a specific BCAA product is unnecessary for anyone consuming the appropriate amount of protein.
- They are also an expensive product to take, so they are NOT recommended.

Greens Powders

- Green powders are a convenient way to increase intake of vitamins, minerals, and antioxidants, especially for athletes who struggle to consume enough fruits and vegetables.
- They are a great product, but should not be a substitute for whole fruits and vegetables, but rather a supplement.
- If the product is from a reputable company, then it could be a good option for those high school athletes that don't like vegetables.

- On the downside, some greens powders are expensive and contain added sugars or artificial ingredients, so be aware.

The primary focus for high school athletes should be on obtaining nutrients from a varied and balanced diet rich in whole foods.

Whole foods offer a complex array of nutrients, fiber, and antioxidants in a natural balance that supplements cannot replicate.

When to Consider Supplements

Supplements may be considered in specific scenarios, such as:

- Dietary restrictions (e.g., vegan athletes might need B12 supplements)
- Living in areas with limited sun exposure (vitamin D supplementation)
- Intense training periods (iron supplements for endurance athletes)

Supplementation should always be approached with caution, especially in young athletes.

It's important to consult with a healthcare provider or a sports nutritionist before starting any supplement regimen.

Which Brand of Supplements Should I Take

Not every product on the shelf at your local vitamin store is approved.

When taking supplements, make sure that they are third party tested and approved.

There are 2 organizations in particular that can provide clarity when choosing products.

Informed Choice
- Informed Choice is an organization that certifies:
  - Sport supplements

- Product ingredients
    - Manufacturing Facilities
- Products that have gone through this certification process have been tested for 146 substances that are prohibited by sport.
- If it has the Informed Choice logo, it has been tested and approved.

NSF Certified for Sport
- This organization provides testing on products to ensure that there are no banned substances.
- This program provides the following information:
    - Annual label claim verification
    - Annual contaminant testing
    - Bi-annual GMP audits for manufacturing

There are a few other organizations that provide third party testing.

The bottom line is, make sure that your product has been verified by a third party before buying.

Supplements can certainly help but they are not magic.

They should never replace a balanced diet, appropriate hydration, and proper training.

CHAPTER 14

| BUILDING THE PLAN

"To eat is a necessity, but to eat intelligently is an art."

– La Rochefoucald

Nutrition for athletes isn't complicated, but it's also not easy.

The challenge will be in the preparation and planning as well as doing what is best, not what is convenient.

Developing a strategy for how many calories and macronutrients an athlete should consume is part of the plan.

Building a nutrition plan requires guidance, a place to begin.

Nutrition plans are not static.

They will change over time, depending on which season an athlete is in.

There are a number of different formulas that can calculate calories and macronutrients for athletes.

This calculator is simple and effective for building a nutrition plan.

CALORIE AND MACRONUTRIENT INTAKE

BUILDING AN ATHLETES NUTRITION PLAN

For those looking to manage weight, use this formula ↓

Manage
Fat: (.35 x bw) x 9 = [ ]
+
Carbs: (2.5 x bw) x 4 = [ ]
+
Protein: (.7 x bw) x 4 = [ ]
=
Total Calories: [ ]

For those looking to increase weight, use this formula ↓

Gain
Fat: (.45 x bw) x 9 = [ ]
+
Carbs: (3.5 x bw) x 4 = [ ]
+
Protein: (1.0 x bw) x 4 = [ ]
=
Total Calories: [ ]

This is a great place to start.

As you can see, the ranges vary depending on whether we are looking to maintain weight or gain weight.

Here is an example of what it would look like for a 150 lbs high school athlete.

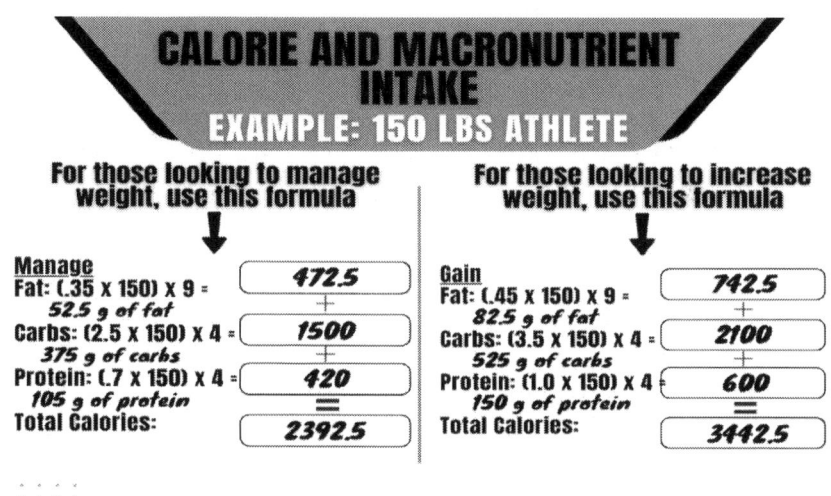

CALORIE AND MACRONUTRIENT INTAKE

EXAMPLE: 150 LBS ATHLETE

For those looking to manage weight, use this formula ↓

Manage
Fat: (.35 X 150) X 9 = [472.5]
52.5 g of fat
+
Carbs: (2.5 X 150) X 4 = [1500]
375 g of carbs
+
Protein: (.7 X 150) X 4 = [420]
105 g of protein
=
Total Calories: [2392.5]

For those looking to increase weight, use this formula ↓

Gain
Fat: (.45 X 150) X 9 = [742.5]
82.5 g of fat
+
Carbs: (3.5 X 150) X 4 = [2100]
525 g of carbs
+
Protein: (1.0 X 150) X 4 = [600]
150 g of protein
=
Total Calories: [3442.5]

As you can see, there is a range of almost 1000 calories between the manage weight and the weight gain athlete.

The macronutrient ranges are listed below.

Protein

- Protein stays consistent all year round.
- Range will be between:
  - *.7 - 1 gram per pound of body weight per day.*
- The goal would be to be closer to the 1 gram per pound of bodyweight.
- This is important for a young athlete, but also as we age to maintain lean muscle mass.

Carbohydrates

- Carbohydrate levels depend on the intensity of the sport.
- If an athlete is at a time of lower intensity, they can start at a lower range then 2.5 x bodyweight.
- For *light activity*, use the following range:
  - *1.5 - 2.5 grams per pound of bodyweight (1.5 x BW = total # of carbs)*
- For *higher intensity activity*, use the following range:
  - *2.5 - 4.5 grams per pound of bodyweight (2.5 x BW = total # of carbs)*
- This will vary over time.
- Signs that you athlete needs more carbohydrates:
  - Easily fatigued
  - Consistent soreness
  - Brain fog

Fats

- Remember, fats won't make you fat unless you over consume.
- They are vital for the health of your body and brain.
- The range for fats will be:
  - 20-25% of an athletes bodyweight

If an athlete is more active, then they will need to consume more calories to keep up with their activity level and recovery.

For athletes looking to gain weight, the offseason is a time to increase calories, but you must monitor that weight gain to make sure it is benefitting you.

We don't want to add significant amounts of body fat just to gain weight.

We want that to be mostly lean muscle, so the gain will be slower overtime.

For most athletes, having a higher percentage of body fat will not benefit them.

We want to maintain our athletic ability, specifically speed and power.

A few markers to evaluate during the process is this:

- Are you gaining, maintaining or losing weight?
  - Based on your desired outcome, proceed as appropriate.
  - Athletes should not have massive fluctuations in weight.
  - Going up or down too quickly is a problem that can eventually lead to injury or illness.
  - Make small, slow changes over time.
- Are you able to maintain your speed?
  - Yes: continue with the plan
  - No: make a small cut in your total calories to decrease body fat.

Body Composition

Body composition is the percentage of our body fat, muscle, bone in our body.

As a teenager, this can be challenging because this is a time when you are going through major changes in your body.

This can be a challenge for high school athletes.

The first thing I want to say is you are more than just your outward appearance.

You have a value and worth that goes beyond the external layers of your body.

Next, I want you to know that being a great athlete doesn't mean you have a six pack.

If having six pack abs and being ripped was a requirement for sports, then bodybuilders would dominate the sporting landscape.

They don't.

Often, bodybuilders have good looking muscles, but poor functioning muscles.

Trying to get a six pack or being ripped can actually cost you.

It may potentially decrease your athleticism and increase your risk of getting injured.

If you are a serious athlete, then you have to understand that how you look is not a factor for determining success.

On the other hand, we don't want to carry too much excess body fat, because that won't help our athletic abilities either.

The goal is to be strong and powerful, while reducing our risk of injury.

This is achieved by feeding ourselves the appropriate amount of calories and macronutrients.

CHAPTER 15

| BE GREAT TODAY

> *"Success is neither magical nor mysterious. Success is the natural consequence of consistently applying the basic fundamentals."*

> \- Jim Rohn

Throughout this book, we have laid out the facts and reasons for building a great nutrition plan.

Returning to the beginning, the main quote that will drive everything is this:

> *"What's simple to do is also simple not to do. The magic is not in the complexity of the task; the magic is in the doing of simple things repeatedly and long enough to ignite the miracle of the Compound Effect."*

We don't lack information.

We lack application.

You have to DO the work.

No one is going to do it for you.

If your goal is to play at your highest level, then you must be the one that is willing to sacrifice the ordinary to become extraordinary!

The difference is that little EXTRA!

Vision

Vision is essential to achieving your full potential.

You need a vision that is so clear it makes you want to get up and do the work in order to allow you to achieve your maximum potential.

"Where there is no vision people will perish, but he that keepeth the law, happy is he." - Proverbs 29:18

I challenged you to create a vision board.

To make something that captures your hopes, dreams and goals.

{Have you started that yet?}

Also, you need something that establishes targets along the way.

You can't go from point A to point Z in one move.

Take time to think about what you need to do in order to accomplish your goals.

Research how much time and effort it will take.

- Yearly goals
- Monthly objectives
- Weekly tasks
- Daily actions

If you have a vision for what you want to achieve, then success becomes a math equation.

You need to accumulate enough hours of deliberate practice in order to achieve success.

Deliberate practice is defined by:

"being effortful in nature, with the main goal of personal improvement of performance rather than enjoyment, and is often performed without immediate reward," K. Anders Ericsson.

Practice doesn't just include the field/ court or the weightroom.

It includes the kitchen.

Eating well and fueling your body for performance is a part of deliberate practice.

Make nutrition a priority, not an afterthought.

Be intentional with your choices rather than just randomly grabbing food.

Focus on what you need to do to be successful, rather than what everyone else is doing.

Choosing your breakfast the night before shows initiative, rather than waking up and staring at the fridge, or trying to sneak out without eating.

Packing your lunch and taking it to school allows you to be in control of your choices, rather than having a choice forced upon you.

Practicing on an empty stomach is not going to allow you to reach your full potential.

Your energy and effort will be down and that can cost your team and yourself.

Skipping your post workout shake or chocolate milk will leave you feeling worse, extend the time you are sore and reduce your ability to recover for the next practice or game.

Athletes, you will be amazed at how much energy you will gain and how much better you will feel if you fuel yourself for performance.

You should be taking more responsibility for your food choices.

Your parents may buy the groceries, but you should be helping in the process of choosing great meals.

The little things matter.

Opportunity is in front of you, but most people don't take full advantage of it.

"Opportunity is missed by most people because it is dressed in overalls and looks like work." – Thomas A. Edison.

If you truly want to achieve BIG goals, then you need to be intentional with your attitude and actions in order to create the life you want.

Chase BIG dreams!

But do it one day at a time!

Go Be Great Today!

Additional Resources

If you have questions after reading this, you can contact Coach Justin through email at: justin@movementfitnessrockford.com

If you are looking for supplements that are third party tested and can help your athlete based on the recommendations I provided in the book, we offer high quality, low cost supplements that we trust. You can go to www.movementfitnesssupplements.com.

Other Books By The Author:

Be Great Today: How to Be Intentional with Your Attitude and Actions to Create Your Best Life.

Have you ever found yourself hitting the snooze button when the alarm goes off?

You roll over and wish you didn't have to start the day.

Have you ever been overweight, out of a job, or looking for hope?

Often, we can find ourselves lost, drifting through each day just trying to survive.

What if you were able to take control of your life?

In *BE GREAT TODAY,* author Justin Kegley takes you through a motivating and inspiring journey to show you how you can CHOOSE to be your best by being intentional with your attitude and actions.

The book details his 100-pound weight loss journey and transformation from Corporate America to being an entrepreneur.

Not only will you get inspired by his message, but you will get a specific and strategic 28-day plan that will help you start living your best life TODAY!

High-Performance Nutrition
HYDRATION
for High School Athletes

Daily Water Goal

- Goal: Drink 100 oz per day
- Minimum Drink 1/2 bodyweight + 15 oz daily.
- Increase water on game/ practice Days
- Track by using a water bottle to fill

2 Hours Prior
- Drink 16 - 20 Ounces

1 Hour Prior
- Drink 8-12 ounces

During Activity
- 3 Big Gulps ever ~15 minutes of water or electrolyte drink
- 5-7 ounces

Post Activity
- Drink 20-24 ounces per pound of bodyweight lost
- Can use an electrolyte drink
- Sodium is a key electrolyte that needs to be replaced following strenuous activity
- Protein and Carbohydrates replacement are key during post activity.
- Using chocolate milk or protein shake as a refuel can be apart of rehydration.

JUSTIN KELLEY COACHING × MOVEMENT FITNESS

High-Performance Nutrition
SLEEP
for High School Athletes

Why Sleep is Important

- Vital for reducing injury risk in athletes.
  - Insufficient sleep is the strongest predictor of injury risk in adolescent athletes
  - 68% decrease in injury risk with 8 hours of sleep.
  - 4 x more injuries occur in players that get 6 hours of sleep v. 9 hours
- Improves Immunity
- Improves Sport Performance
- Increases Mental Clarity
- Reduces Stress
- Increases Reaction Time

Sleep Strategies

- Set Bed Time
- No Electronics in Room
  - Room is for relaxing/ sleeping
  - No phone / TV
- Room Setting
  - Dark as possible
  - Temperature between 62-68 Degrees
  - Reduce Noise
- Create a Wind down routine
  - Shower
  - Relaxation / Breathing
  - Reduce stress
- No Caffeine 8 hours before bed
  - Caffeine is NOT recommended for anyone under 18!
- Try not to have consecutive nights of 8 hours or less

Daily Sleep Goal
- 8-10 Hours

High-Performance Nutrition
NUTRITION
for High School Athletes

Daily Nutrition Goals
- Eat protein at every meal
- Breakfast fuels the day
  - Protein
  - Healthy Fats
  - Carbohydrates (starchy)
- Fill energy stores before activity
- Immediately replenish after activity
  - Protein
  - Carbohydrates
- Eat at home more then out

4+ Hours Prior
- Eat a Full Meal
  - Pasta with Marinara & Roll
  - Fruit & Yogurt
  - Grilled Chicken Breast, baked potato & broccoli

2+ Hours Prior
- Eat a Heavy Snack
  - Bagel w/ Peanut Butter & Banana
  - Greek Yogurt & Berries w/ Granola

1-2 Hours Prior
- Eat a Light Snack with more carbs
  - Fruit
    - banana
    - apple
  - Low Fat Yogurt
  - Mini bagel w/ Peanut Butter

Less than 1 Hour
- Less food, more fluids
  - 8-14 OZ Low Fat Chocolate Milk
  - 12-20 oz Electrolyte Drink

References

Mohr, Chris. *Certified Sports Nutrition Coaches' Manual.* National Sports Performance Association, 2017.

Berardi, John & Andrews, Ryan. *The Essentials of Sport and Exercise Nutrition.* Precision Nutrition, 2013.

Cain, Brian. *Mental Performance Mastery Coaches Certification Course Training Manual.* Brian Cain Peak Performance, LLC, February 2022.

Walter Science School, *The Water In You: Water and the Human Body.* https://www.usgs.gov/special-topics/water-science-school/science/water-you-water-and-human-body#:~:text=Up%20to%2060%25%20of%20the,bones%20are%20watery%3A%2031%25, May 22, 2019

Johnson, Brittany. Omega-3's: *Why they are the real alphas of fat for athletic performance.* Science for Sport, Mar 2, 2023. https://www.scienceforsport.com/omega-3s-why-they-are-the-real-alphas-of-fat-for-athletic-performance/#:~:text=Omega%2D3s%20contain%20anti%2Dinflammatory,exercise%20muscle%20damage%20and%20soreness

Woodward, Emily & Mercer, Amber. *Omega-3 fatty acid supplementation for concussions.* SportSafe, https://www.sportssafect.com/blog/omega-3-fatty-acid-supplementation-for-concussions#:~:text=Our%20%E2%80%9Comega%2D3%20deficiency%20puts,improve%20communication%20between%20nerve%20cells.

Final Note:

I want to say thank you to my wife Theresa.

Without her, none of this would be possible!

I am so grateful to have you as my partner in life!

I Love You!

To my boys, Riley, Cooper and Colton.

Thank you for making my life better.

I am so thankful that GOD gave me the three of you!

I could not be more proud of each of you.

TO YOU: THE READER

My hope is that this book helps you to achieve your goals.

More importantly though, I pray that you would know that there is a GOD that loves you and desires a relationship with you.

He created you and has amazing things planned for you if you are open to his calling.

"For God so loved the world, that he gave his only begotten Son, that whosoever believeth in him should not perish, but have everlasting life."

- John 3:16

Made in the USA
Columbia, SC
19 May 2025

58190989R00078